BRAZILIAN JIU-JITSU

THE PATH to the BLACK BELT

Rodrigo Gracie and Kid Peligro

INVISIBLE CITIES PRESS • MONTPELIER, VERMONT

Rodrigo thanks his friend Ron Bergum
and American Home Mortgage
for the support over the years.

Invisible Cities Press
50 State Street
Montpelier, VT 05602
www.invisiblecitiespress.com

Cataloging-in-Publication Data available from the Library of Congress

ISBN 1-931229-42-2

Anyone practicing the techniques in this book does so at his or her own risk. The authors
and the publisher assume no responsibility for the use or misuse of information contained
in this book or for any injuries that may occur as a result of practicing the techniques contained herein. The illustrations and text are for informational purposes only. It is imperative to practice these holds and techniques under the strict supervision of a qualified
instructor. Additionally, one should consult a physician before embarking on any demanding physical activity.

Printed in the United States

Book design by Peter Holm, Sterling Hill Productions
Edited by Tia McCarthy and Carmine Grimaldi, Invisible Cities Press

CONTENTS

Takedowns

Guard Defense Basics

Sweeps and Reversals

INTRODUCTION

Anyone who has ever started practicing a martial art knows that achieving Black Belt is the ultimate goal. The first day you walk into an academy, you know that your objective is eventually to become a Black Belt. This can sometimes cause people to place too much emphasis on belt progression and cause them to lose focus on the most important goal, which is, of course, becoming proficient in the martial art.

And while belt systems can become too much of a focus for some people, they do play an important role in marital arts, and particularly in Gracie Jiu-Jitsu. They help differentiate between various technical levels and also represent, and reward, the student's effort, sacrifice, dedication and achievement.

There are five belts for adults in Gracie Jiu-Jitsu: White, Blue, Purple, Brown and Black. Traditionally, students progressed and achieved the next belt on merit and technical proficiency, after they had spent immense amounts of time training on the mat, thinking and preparing for the training times. While many practitioners have access to good instruction from a qualified Black Belt, many areas still lack qualified teachers, leaving the student wanting to find additional information on how best to train in order to reach their ultimate goal, the Black Belt.

While no book can turn you into a Black Belt, books can give you useful knowledge and guidance. The purpose of this book is to supplement your instructor's lessons and, by giving you additional information, help you reach your goal faster, better and more efficiently.

By following the instruction and insights provided in *Path to the Black Belt*, any Gracie Jiu-Jitsu practitioner – no matter how experienced – should be able to increase their understanding of the art and become better acquainted with the intricacies of Jiu-Jitsu.

Additionally, the techniques selected and presented in this book will provide a solid foundation that, if fully assimilated, practiced, and properly executed, will be enough to catapult you to the Black Belt.

What to look for in class and in an instructor so you can achieve your personal goals
Selecting a school and an instructor is one of the most important decisions that you can make when beginning any martial art. This is particularly true in Gracie Jiu-Jitsu because of the training's intensity, the extreme physical contact and the art's complexity.

While there are many factors that can influence your decision in selecting a school and an instructor, we would like to point out several important ones.

First and foremost, focus on the quality of instruction. A great instructor is not simply defined as having great technical knowledge, but also by his ability to work with the class, relating to the students, conducting the class and managing the relationships between the students.

While there's no substitute for great technical knowledge, the instructor's knowledge is as important as the way that he conveys and transmits it to his students. A very impressive competition resumé is valueless if the instructor can't explain to his students the techniques that he uses and the reasons that he uses them. Of course, success in competitions generally means that your instructor is capable of using his techniques efficiently against top-level opponents, and that certainly adds to the value of his information. Additionally, try to avoid those instructors who aren't flexible with the lessons, imposing their style rather than allowing you to discover your own personal methods.

You need to define your personal objectives in learning Jiu-Jitsu. Ask yourself:

- Do you want to learn to protect yourself?
- Do you want to learn the sport aspects of the art?
- Do you want to be a top competitor?

Be honest when you answer these questions and then evaluate your situation and see which type of school you fits you best. One personal factor that may affect your decision is your profession; if you need to use your hands to make a living - like a surgeon or a dentist - you may not want to pursue a competition career. If you don't have time or energy after work to fully participate in a demanding and tough sparring school, you need to be honest with yourself and look for a school that fits you best.

Different instructors will focus on different aspects of the art. The instructor's personality will generally influence both the way that he conducts the class and the school's general focus. Some schools are focused on competition, some on self-defense, some on street fighting or NHB, while others work more at fostering a well-rounded fighter. It's important that you seriously and honestly evaluate your personal objectives. Do you want to learn Jiu-Jitsu to become a great competitor and rise to champion? Do you want to learn self-defense? Are you going to take Gracie Jiu-Jitsu because you want to learn a martial art for personal development? Or do you just want a hobby to stay fit? Depending on your answer, you should look for a school that best fits your personal objectives. It doesn't make any sense for you to join a school that focuses on competition if you're mainly interested in self-defense. Similarly, if you want to become a champion fighter, joining a school that focuses on self-defense would not help you very much. If you are a high energy person who wants to spar hard, then you should look for a school that matches your style; if you're a surgeon who wants to learn Jiu-Jitsu but can't hurt himself, look for a school that specializes in controlled training.

School atmosphere is another important aspect that you should pay attention to when selecting an academy. Since you are going to spend a great deal of time learning your techniques and sparring with team-mates, the academy needs to be a place in which you feel comfortable. It needs to be fun; you should feel a desire to attend class and work with your teammates. If your teammates aren't like friends and the academy as a whole isn't like an extended family, chances are high that you'll eventually fade out of the sport. If you don't trust your teammates, or they don't share the same bond with you, then the school is just not for you.

It is very important that the instructor controls the conduct of spar-ring, particularly how the pairs are matched up. In general, good instructors will pair up people of the same technical level, size, age group and style (i.e. aggressive, reckless, passive). When people are correctly matched, they can challenge each other's technical level without a large difference in power and stamina. If you see people of largely different sizes constantly being paired up, or if the instructor simply allows anyone to pair with anyone, you should take it as a warning sign. Many times, larger and younger people are more aggressive and can cause injuries when training against smaller, weaker or older people.

As a general rule, students with matching traits should be paired together, allowing them to challenge each other while diminishing the chances of injury and frustration. If you have an older surgeon constantly paired up with a young marine, you're not only risking the surgeon's well-being, but you're also forcing him to endure beatings from a younger and more aggressive partner. We once had a student in our school who was a dentist. He was very good at Jiu-Jitsu and wanted to test himself against all different opponents. Obviously, in his case, his hands were of great value, so while we allowed him to train with most people, we kept some of the larger and most reckless students away from him. This way, he was protected not only from dangerous opponents, but also from his own personality that drove him to test his limits. If he had been allowed to train with anyone in the school, he may have injured his hands and lost the ability to earn an income. But more fundamentally, he would have been frustrated; at his level of training, he wouldn't be able to survive against the bigger and younger students of the academy. As his technical proficiency increased, he was allowed to fight a greater range of partners, but we always kept his personal situation in mind. If he runs into a problem on the streets and needs to fight a stronger, younger and bigger opponent, he would have no choice but to fight; his adrenaline and technical knowledge would most likely equalize the battle. But it makes no sense to make him test himself everyday at the academy! The chances of getting injured are too great, particularly in light of the small impact it would have on his progression.

School location is the final deciding factor. Don't take distance and convenience too lightly. If your school is so far away from your house that you have to spend an inordinate amount of time to reach it, chances are you'll stop training after a short while. All things being somewhat equal, select a school that is convenient for you to get to. This way, you will find less excuses to skip class, and furthermore, you'll be able to go even when your schedule is tighter than usual. By selecting a school that is near you, you'll definitely give yourself added incentive to train more frequently and greatly increase your chances of progressing in the art.

Drills

Drills are a very important yet often overlooked aspect of learning Gracie Jiu-Jitsu. It is much more fun to spar and go against a training partner in the academy than to work on perfecting a move by repeating it over and over but there is a lot to gain by repetition. Olympic Judo athletes drill much more often than they train. When you spar, you increase the chances of injury. Because of this, Olympic fighters practice the position over and over, often one hundred times per side, until they have it down. After some time and repetition, they start to do the position automatically; they have trained both their body and mind, allowing them to properly execute the technique. When the time comes to use this move, you'll execute it much faster and with much more precision than if you had skipped practicing the technique and had just sparred all the time.

Rodrigo: "When I'm teaching my students, one of the techniques that I use to improve their ability in learning the move's essence is to tire them out before I even show them a drill. I put them through the warm up, show them a technique and then, once they are tired, I get them to do a drill. When they're tired, they need to rely on technical perfection, rather than power and explosiveness, in order to repeat the drill over and over. This way, they not only learn the drill, but they learn how to do it effortlessly because the technique has been absorbed by the subconscious."

For instance, you may not like to pass the guard toreana style because you're not confident in the technique and, when you use it, it doesn't come out right. Your instructor may show you a drill or two that work with this style of pass and have you repeat it 10 or 20 times before each class for a few weeks. After that you will get better at the toreana pass and will not only start using it more, but gain confidence in it! The average student learns a new technique, practices it once or twice, and then tries to use it in sparring—that is simply not going to work. The judoka learns a takedown and then practices it over and over; many times he will practice the set-up of the takedown repeatedly. He'll practice it about a hundred times before he even completes one throw. By the time he has the opportunity to use the throw in a fight or in sparring, he has the movement down and is ready to execute it perfectly. To take another example, a kick-boxer, or muay-thai fighter, will hit the pads with punches and kicks many times over before he ever tries one of the strikes in a sparring match.

The point is that you have to perfect the move to the point that you can execute it automatically - without even thinking – before you can successfully use it in a fighting or sparring match. Unfortunately, most jiu-jitsu practitioners don't do that. At times, it's because the instructor doesn't encourage practicing, instead getting them to spar right away, at other times it's just because sparring is way more fun than repetition training. But this style of training will greatly hinder your progress to the coveted Black Belt.

FIGURE 1

Specific training drills

Specific training is good because you can practice a situation over and over; something that may not happen in sparring but once or twice a day. For instance, you may begin the training session mounted on someone. Your objective is to submit him. This will help you concentrate on the submissions and, if he escapes, you can start over. This way, you can develop your submission skills from the mounted position without fear of losing the position. Compare this to a regular sparring session - you start inside someone's guard, then you make all this effort to pass the guard, reach side control and then finally mount the person (figures 1 through 4). In this scenario, you'd be very reluctant to try anything in fear that you'd lose the position to an upa and end up on the bottom.

Controlled specific training is a great way to avoid injuries. Since the objectives and restrictions of the training session are spelled out

FIGURE 2

FIGURE 3

FIGURE 4

before the actual training begins, the practitioners will generally work under more control than usual sparring sessions and thus avoid injury. Rodrigo: "I had a student who was an office worker and he came from another school where he was always getting hurt because of uncontrolled sparring. When he came to me, he was seriously thinking of quitting Jiu-Jitsu, as he could not afford the down time from work and was tired of missing class because of his injuries. Instead of forcing him to face anyone in the academy, and perhaps driving him out of the sport, I made use of controlled specific training to bring him back into training shape, build up his confidence in his abilities and take away the fear of getting hurt. After a while, he was back and training regularly. And he still trains to this day."

Instructor awareness

If your instructor doesn't account for students' particular needs, you need to be extra aware and use your best judgment in selecting the best techniques for your body type. Rodrigo Gracie: "I started training in Gracie Jiu-Jitsu with my father, Reylson Gracie at the Gavea shopping mall. My dad's system is more focused on self-defense; it is directed towards the normal person that isn't concerned with competing in a sports Jiu-Jitsu tournament. Rather, he wanted to be able to defend himself and his family in the event of an aggressive attack on the streets. His system is directed towards the normal individual, a person without special athletic abilities that wants to learn the art.

"I got my Black Belt at 18 years old. My father moved to America and opened a school in Corona del Mar, California. When I came, I started teaching there and continued for two years. After that, I returned to Brazil, but my dad moved to Las Vegas and I decided to return and help him there. I learned a lot about teaching from him."

As an instructor, Rodrigo believes it is important to teach the student a technique in a way that he can adapt to his body type and style. It is a mistake for the instructor to try to teach the student just the things he will be good at, or that the instructor likes. A good instructor, and this is something that Rodrigo tries to do, is the one that teaches techniques that he doesn't use regularly, realizing that they may work well for certain students. In other words, a good instructor should search through his techniques and try to tailor lessons to the individual person, to his abilities and shortcomings. He should look for the techniques that will work best for each individual student. And the student, after a while, gets to understand what is best for him, which techniques work best for his personal characteristics.

As a student, you need to be aware of your personal characteristics and, while keeping an open mind for all techniques, select, after some time, which ones are best for you. You will be able to recognize what it was that made a certain move difficult for you. Once you isolate the reason, it may help to avoid other techniques that will give you the same problems. Concentrate on the things that work best for your style and body, and find those characteristics that help you progress. For instance, if you're not the fastest person in the world, you should select the moves that don't require a lot of speed for success. Instead, look for the ones that require steady development. For example, the toreana guard pass (figure 5) requires more quickness than the tight underhooking of the leg pass (figure 6). So if you are a quick person, the toreana will be better for you, and conversely, if you're a slow fighter, the underhook is the better pass for you.

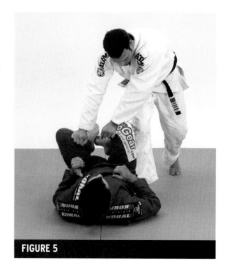
FIGURE 5

Proper pace in learning the techniques

It's crucial for the student to be patient. Many times, the new student, in his rush for progress and knowledge, wants to learn a lot of new positions and techniques. It's important for the instructor to be aware of the student's impatience and not teach him a technique that he's not mature enough to fully understand and apply. For instance, Rodrigo won't teach a new student a butterfly sweep; until he's more developed, he won't know how to move his body correctly and get in the proper position. Additionally, that new student won't face a situation where the advanced technique works, so he will quickly forget it. Similarly, it's important for the student to have patience until he is prepared to advance in his training. He must first focus on his current batch of techniques until they become second nature. At that point, the student is ready to learn another move, or a series of moves in a careful sequence. Many times, students complain that the instructor is "hiding" his techniques or not "showing the good stuff", when in reality, the student is not ready for the new information. If he were presented with these complex moves, it would just add confusion to an already difficult regimen.

FIGURE 6

In Gracie Jiu-Jitsu, the student needs to learn a technique, be able to properly execute it, and then be able to decide which technique is necessary for each stance during a fight. For instance, in boxing, the fighters are always standing up and can only hit above the waist. Likewise, in kickboxing, the fight also happens standing up and, even though the fighters can hit anywhere, there are a limited number of strikes. In contrast to this, Gracie Jiu-jitsu allows for many different positions; both fighters can be standing, one can be standing while the other is on the ground, both can be on the ground, or they can even be upside down – the plane of action is limited only by the ground, allowing for an incredible number of variables. As if playing a game of high-speed chess, the new practitioner not only has to deal with all these factors, but also has to be able to select the right technique and properly execute it.

Don't get hurt!

Many Gracie Jiu-Jitsu practitioners have had an injury of some kind during their career. Of those, a large number end up quitting, either because they reincur the same injury, or they get new injuries. They start to worry more about being injured and the fun of training begins to dry up. If every three or four months, you have to stop training because you get injured, you may eventually give up. No one wants to go around getting injured all the time! So it's important to remember that protecting yourself during training and identifying mistakes - like technical misunderstandings or over-training - are two of the keys necessary in fulfilling your ultimate dream of becoming a Black Belt.

Protecting yourself during training

It is ultimately up to you to protect yourself during training. Although ideally, it's always best for you and your partner to worry about each other's safety, in the real world, you shouldn't count on anyone but yourself to worry about a bad position or about getting a limb stuck somewhere. Instead of worrying about escaping a position - even when one of your arms, fingers or legs is stuck in a dangerous or awkward position - you should first consider how to best protect yourself from injury. Many times, you can give up a position in order to release the limb, or you may have to bump or, if nothing else works, you can just tell your partner to stop, get him to fix the danger and continue sparring from the same position. For example, let's say you're defending the guard, your foot gets stuck in the opponent's gi and is in danger of being twisted if he moves in a certain way. Just yell: "Stop!" and release the foot from the gi, reposition your foot to the position it should be in and continue the training. The only other option is to hope for the best and possibly end up with a hyper-extended ankle and a wasted month of recovery.

Don't let your pride get in the way of your training. Often, students are too proud to submit and end up injured. Remember that training takes time and you can learn from every submission.

Identifying mistakes

Ask yourself "Am I over-training?" You are if you train when you are exhausted or sick. At times, the desire to train is so strong that you will want to train every day. And on top of that, because you realize that if you are stronger and in better condition, you will be able to last longer in sparring, you will also want to increase your conditioning along with the Jiu-Jitsu training. After a while, your body will get tired and ask you to stop and rest. But your desire to improve is too strong and you insist on continuing your exhaustive regimen. Soon, you're mentally *and* physically tired while you are hitting the mats. At this point, you're a prime candidate for getting injured. Although you may think that the quantity of time on the mat is the key to progress, resting your body is also a big part of the equation. When you feel the signs of over-training, like really sore muscles, fatigue and aching joints, your body is telling you to take a rest. If you refuse to listen to it, you will most likely get injured. It's similar to the oil light turning on in your car. You can either stop and take care of the engine, or you can pull the light out and ignore the warning signs. If you choose the latter, your engine will eventually give out on you.

Resting the body will also allow you to rest your mind. Since Jiu-Jitsu is like a chess match, you are constantly using your brain. Your brain is needed to make lightening-fast decisions, like which technique to use against you opponent's incessantly changing counter-techniques. But your mind is not only put under stress when imminent danger of a submission is upon you, but also when you're excited about securing the finishing hold against a good opponent. If you constantly overtax your mind, you will expose yourself to injuries; if your mind is dull, you may not realize that something is wrong and that you are about to twist a limb, or that you need to move to protect your foot that is dangerously caught in the mat.

With a rested mind, you will feel fresh and ready to train every time you hit the mats. With a rested body and sharp mind, you'll get a lot more out of training and be able to perform at your best level, and, most important, avoid getting injured!

If you do get injured

No matter how well you try to protect yourself, injuries will eventually occur. They're part of any sport, especially in martial arts where the physical contact and constant interaction between two fighters will at times create unexpected situations that could end in injury.

Since injuries are inevitable in any martial art, the question is not only how to avoid injury, but also what to do once you get injured. When injured, students will oftentimes get anxious about their progress and want to quickly get back to the mats, rushing and returning prematurely. The result is another injury or re-injury to same area. After a few injuries and several times away from the mats, the student will most likely become discouraged and quit. When you are injured, you need to rest, protect your body and allow it to heal properly before you come back and start training again. Additionally, when you return to the mats, make sure that you begin slowly and allow for your body to readjust to the rigors of training. Don't return and try to pick up where you left off! Be smart, ease up on your return and soon you will be right back to the old speed, or maybe even better. Many times, people have found that with proper rest and treatment, they not only quickly come back, but they actually improve from the rest. Now, don't get us wrong—we're not advocating that you get injured so you can get better, but rather pointing out how rest and proper usage of your down time will keep you sharp.

What should you do in the meantime when faced with an injury? If you're not able to perform at all, you should try to visualize your moves and imagine that you're sparring, watch videos of competition and go observe your regular class so that you can keep your mind on the training and the techniques.

If you can move your body and execute some techniques, you may be able to go to the academy and do some controlled drills and position repetition. Talk to your instructor about working on a technique that doesn't tax your injury; try it thirty times to each side.

Learn how to train

The first time that you train Jiu-Jitsu, you might get addicted to it; this might make you train extra hard for the first week, and then for the second, third and fourth week. By the month's end, you will have trained so hard that you managed to get injured. But you still love it and think about it all the time. And you can't sleep, thinking instead about the techniques. They stay in your every thought. But no matter how tempting it may be to push yourself, you have to train intelligently. Achieving the Black Belt is not that difficult; Jiu-Jitsu is not that difficult. What's difficult is the Jiu-Jitsu being taught today specifically for competition. Because a lot of people begin with competitive Jiu-Jitsu, they think that they can never achieve Black Belt. Think about it, take a sport like Judo—how many Judo practitioners are there? A lot. And how many people actually reach the Olympics in Judo? Only a very small portion! The point is you don't need to practice like you're going to be the World Champion in order to reach Black Belt. You just need to learn the aspects of Gracie Jiu-Jitsu that are important to you and to your instructor; to learn the parts that are fun, the parts that get you fit, the parts that will help you defend yourself and your family in a street fight and the parts that are integral to learning the martial art.

It's important that the instructor differentiates you from a professional athlete. There are different standards for different people — a young competitor should be judged differently than a middle-aged professional. If you are being compared to the top fighters in the school, or to the teacher himself, then you are in the wrong school and may never achieve your goal. There are many schools where the level for advancement is measured by being able to surpass all the students of the same belt in the school, but that doesn't work in real life. If you are smaller, weaker, older, or slower than your training partners of a similar technical level, then they will regularly beat you! To progress and reach Black Belt, you need to develop efficiency in your techniques and be able to defend yourself by applying the right techniques at the right time.

FIGURE 7

Am I training correctly?

Many times, we let our egos get in the way of learning. Human beings are natural competitors, particularly in sports and even more so in martial arts. We tend to view any one-on-one practice as a means to gauge our progress. That can be counter-productive. If you go to your academy and try to bring a trophy home every practice day, you are training incorrectly. The point of sparring and academy training is to learn and to progress, not to win at every training session. If you're sparring with a win-at-all-costs attitude, you're better off competing. At a school you're supposed to be helping each other like a family and not competing with each other. Sparring is the time to learn and to improve; if you're being submitted but are learning and progressing every time, then you're better off than if you never submitted but were incapable of advancing in applying your techniques.

FIGURE 8

Additionally, if you fight so hard that you win by submission, and you specifically battle each time to finish your opponent at every opportunity, you may also be hindering your progress. The main reason is that if you battle every time with the single objective of defeating your sparring partner, he will sense the feeling and will fight with the same intensity in order to get you back. In this case, what should be an educational and friendly sparring session turns into a fight for survival. If your partner doesn't want to fight back every time, then he might stop sparring with you—not everyone wants to fight for their life every time they step on the mat. You stand to gain much more in every sense by allowing your sparring to flow. Suppose you get near a submission - let's say an arm-lock from the guard (figure 7) - to the point that you know you have better than an 80% chance of success. It's much better for you to allow him to escape (figures 8, 9 and 10) and see what his reaction is so that you can build off it, than to fight with all your energy for the arm-lock just to please your ego. You stand to gain a lot more by allowing your opponent to escape; it's best

FIGURE 9

FIGURE 10

to see how he escapes and follow with a counter, fine-tuning your sequences rather than single-mindedly fighting for the initial move.

When you allow your partner to escape, your training flows and you can go through ten times as many situations than you would if you fought hard for every position. By following this system, you make the training much more challenging and fun, and you go through a much greater percentage of your technical arsenal. And the same goes for your partner. He will be able to practice many more situations, have much more fun and feel more challenged and invigorated at the end of the session than he would if he harbored hard feelings.

If your instructor encourages his students to fight with each other all the time, you either have a school that is totally directed towards competition, or you have a school with very few students because so many of them get hurt and quit!

If every time you go to the academy, you wonder 'Who will make me tap?", "Who will I make tap?", or think, "Darn, I got tapped by so and so, I need to get even", then your road towards that ultimate goal is going to be very difficult. If you are submitted, the proper thing is to ask the partner or instructor what you did wrong and, instead of trying to get even, try to correct your mistakes so you don't repeat them.

Instructors also play a big part in the atmosphere and intensity of the training; they are, of course, greatly responsible for the progress and mental attitudes of their students. Students try to emulate their instructors; if the instructor has a bad attitude, the students may develop one, too. Take this scenario: There is a student that is a professional, works in an office eight hours a day, loves to train and wants to train with all the other students. At times, he loses and at times he wins, but he always has fun sparring, regardless of the results. Which do you think is better for healthy progress: If his teacher discourages him from training because "You are a Brown Belt, you shouldn't be losing to Blue Belts," or if the teacher says, "Good job, the only thing is, I noticed that you tapped because you did this wrong. Next time you should do this!" Of course, the second instructor will be better for the students; they will progress and learn because he encourages them to not only not worry about winning or losing, but points out the mistakes that the students make and shows how to correct them.

How do regular students improve?
If you're a regular person who holds a steady job, maybe you have a family and no immediate aspirations of becoming a World Champion, then the following should be your guide:

1. Make sure that you train regularly: This might seem simple enough, but if you don't train, you won't get better. If you don't train at least twice a week, preferably three times, your timing and execution will not improve; you'll only see the moves when you're readjusting your belt, minutes after you've tapped. Stay consistent with your training.

2. You need to train with other regular persons like you: training with the top fighters in the school will definitely help, but it's only when you train with people that are equal or worse than you that you can realistically realize your potential and see your real difficulties—when you train against the best of the best, the results are usually the same: you're going to lose.

3. You need to be in some shape, not top shape, but at least regular to good training shape so that you can last more than five minutes in a sparring session during class. Make sure you are able and fit enough to have an effective training in which your reactions and breathing are still strong enough to allow you to function well instead of being so tired that you can't properly react and protect yourself. The knowledge you gain as you train will go a long way to helping you to relax and last longer in practice.

4. You need to repeat the moves that you learn several times. And since there's limited training time, you should focus on the moves that you want to be good at, making them the most commonly occurring and most effective moves in your repertoire. With repetition, your technique will greatly improve.

5. You need to be able to link two, and preferably three moves to every position. For example: The upa (figure 11) followed by the elbow escape works better than using just one or the other. On the attack side, the arm-lock, triangle and omoplata sequence from the guard is extremely effective. Combining techniques will force your opponents to spend a lot of energy and trick him into falling into your trap. Again, because of your limited time, you need to limit the combos that you learn and practice; but remember, there are some that are so important that you need to have them down to be able to effectively train.

FIGURE 11

6. Finally, and most importantly, you need to have fun when you train. If you enjoy your training you will get better.

How do competitors improve?

Although we do not believe that competing is a prerequisite to achieving the Black Belt, competition does have its benefits for those who are willing to participate in it. While competing will help you deal with your emotions and other factors, preparing for the competition is arguably the most important part of the equation - and it gives the most benefits.

While Gracie Jiu-Jitsu sparring is extremely close to a real fight, competition, because of the personal commitment by both athletes, is even closer. When faced with a tournament match, the competitor faces all the emotions of a real fight, plus a few added elements. Since he knows that his opponent should have the same amount of knowledge and competency as he does (or better), the doubts and fears come out and have to be confronted before, and right up to the minute of the match. It's not uncommon for even the best fighters to have so much anxiety before a big event that they can't even sleep the night before. Some top fighters have been known to wear their competition gi the day before the event and some even sleep in it — the high emotional stress involved in tournament fighting not only helps you prepare for other tournaments, but also for life's extreme situations, such as business, jobs or familial pressure.

But the fears and anticipation of competition are just a part of the benefits that you get when you set the goal of competing. The preparation and specific training for the event, if done properly, will greatly propel your game.

But how do you prepare for an event? There are several aspects that need to be addressed: first, you need to be in great conditioning shape and be able to fight one or more fights without even trying; second, your game needs to be at its best, built on a solid basis of techniques; and third, it's preferable to have a strategy when you go into each match.

Conditioning

Depending on what belt you are, there will be different time limits for a fight. Generally speaking, tournaments follow the IBJJF rules; the adult divisions are as follows:

Blue Belt - 6 minutes
Purple Belt – 7 minutes
Brown Belt - 8 minutes
Black Belt – 10 minutes

Assuming that you are fighting in a regular event, you can expect one to three matches for the day, and more if you're fighting both the weight division and the absolute or open weight division, or if the tournament is very small. You need to prepare your body to retain some juice for the last fights, keeping in mind that, as you advance in the tournament, the fighters will get tougher. There are many books dealing with training and preparation for Jiu-Jitsu. Rodrigo's cousin Royce has a very good one called *Superfit*. Look for a personal trainer or follow a reliable book routine, making sure that you are physically ready to do your best on the day of the event. Nothing takes more way from a fighter than when he knows that he's not physically ready to fight!

Technical training

Technical preparation for a tournament is different from everyday training. Generally speaking, one tries to improve the areas that they are good at, while finding ways to hide their weaker side. The winner of the most matches is the one that is best at bringing the game to his strengths while avoiding his weaknesses. Avoid learning new moves a few days before competition. Practice your normal game and the things you do best. Refine what you already know.

In preparing for a tournament, you will find that some of the most effective drills are those in which you have a short time span (one or two minutes) in which you need to perform a specific task and, if you are successful, you should restart and repeat it as many times as possible within the time frame. For example:

A. Start with a partner mounted on you. Try to escape while your partner tries to maintain the position and submit you (or the other way around).
B. Start with the opponent in your closed guard and either submit or sweep him (or the other way around).
C. Start with the opponent in another good offensive position. Try to escape while your partner tries to submit you (or the other way around).
D. Any other specific drill.

Another great way to improve your competition game is to have simulated matches with referees and points. And to even further increase your awareness of a match, try varying the situation, such as two minutes to go and you're down four points. It's extremely important to tailor your sparring session to the regulation time, so if you're a purple belt, you should spar seven minute rounds. This way, you become accustomed to the length of the matches and will naturally acquire a mental time clock, which will tell you to speed up or slow down depending on the situation.

Strategy preparation

Strategy is the last step in proper competition preparation. Many fights are won or lost because of strategy. At the highest levels, where the technique and conditioning are somewhat equal, the main difference is strategy. But even at the lower competition levels, strategy can play an important part in achieving good results.

Strategy involves fight planning, emotional control and time management. The simplest aspect of fight planning involves observing your opponent fight, and knowing his strengths and weaknesses as well as you know your own. Once that's complete, try to bring the fight to your strong points while avoiding your weak ones. For example, if your standing game is strong, you may want to keep the fight in the standing position and focus on getting the takedown points. If your passing game is stronger than your bottom game, one of your main goals should be trying to fight from the top rather than from the bottom. Of course, often we can't control the match and have to deal with the ever-changing situation that is present during the match. A good game plan gives you an ideal road map to follow, rather than proceeding without any direction or objective. The person who can bring the fight to his game plan generally wins.

Emotional control can be developed by competing frequently; with each match, and with each competition, you will develop the ability to perform at your highest level, without wasting any energy through nervousness, anxiety and other draining emotions. Ideally, before, during and after the match, you should feel, think and act the same way as you do when sparring in the academy. Experience in tournament fighting will greatly strengthen your emotional control.

In the match, it's you against your opponent, for a limited amount of time. Time management is a very important aspect; many fights have been won and lost by mere points, so a successful fighting strategy that accounts for the time limits of a match is crucial. Top competitors develop a sense for the match times and constantly pay attention to both the score and time, adapting their fighting strategy during the match to fit with the score/time equation. The drilling you do in your technical preparation for a tournament is key in developing your strategic approach. Through drilling, you will learn which moves or sequences of moves take the most time for you to accomplish – and which are fastest for you. If you only have a few seconds left in a match, and you're down by just a couple of points, knowing what you need to execute to get ahead can make the difference between winning and losing. If you are down by a small point differential you may only need a reversal to get ahead. However if you are behind by a large point differential and time is running out you may have to take greater risks in order to achieve a submission.

Learning a new technique

A situation that occurs often, and is a great hindrance to progress, is the process of learning a new technique. A typical situation is as follows: Your instructor shows you a new technique. After a few tries of practicing it with your sparring partner, you have the basic mechanics of the move down and immediately think, "Great! I'll use this new move on the next victim that lines up in front of me!"

The plan is well laid out; you've learned a new technique - one that most people don't know - and you're ready to spring it out on your unsuspecting training partner. The plan worked well… until you actually started to do it! Then every time you tried the new move, your partner would do something that you weren't counting on, getting the advantage and placing you in a bad position. Soon enough, you decide the move was no good and that it would be best to move on and learn something else. The only fault with your logic was that, immediately after your next sparring partner was your instructor, who proceeded to pull off the same move against you every time—no matter how hard you tried to use the same counter that your previous partner had just used against you! Has something like this happened to you before? If it has, here is a little help:

Trying to apply a technique in a sparring or fighting situation immediately after you learn it is bound to end in failure—you haven't learned the technique well enough! Sounds confusing? Well it is. Even though you have the basic mechanics of a move down, it doesn't mean that you have the understanding, the knowledge, and especially the timing of execution. When you apply a new technique, 90% of the time it won't work, particularly if you are going against someone of equal or better skill than you.

So how do you learn a technique if you can't use it in training? Don't use it in sparring just yet! First, to increase the odds of success, and to learn the intricacies of a new technique, you should drill it several times against a willing partner. By doing this, you'll get the mechanics of the move down pat and be able to apply it correctly. Second, you need to learn to identify the right moment to apply the technique. To do this, start trying the new move against someone lighter and less skilled than you. With someone less skilled, you'll be able to try the move several times without much consequence, allowing you to figure out when it works, when it doesn't and what happens when it doesn't! Third, and most important, keep mental notes when the move works best—did you feign a different move to set it up, or did you wait for your partner to place his weight in a certain way? By noting when the technique worked best, you'll start to develop a mental trigger for that specific move. Finally, once you have all those down, try to emulate the same situations as when the move worked.

How to select the best techniques for you

While there isn't a technique that won't work for everybody, we naturally have preferences and styles. In the initial stages of learning, your task is to follow the instructor's lessons and absorb all the techniques that are shown to you in class. However, as you progress in the sport, your instincts and personality will greatly influence how your game develops. There will be techniques and parts of the game that you understand and absorb quickly, and other parts that are more difficult. While you should concentrate on developing all phases of your game, you may selectively shy away from certain parts that are most difficult, concentrating instead on parts that naturally seem to fit you best.

While we're not condoning complete abandonment of any part of the fighting game, realistically you can progress quite far if you manage to solidify certain areas of your game and can direct your opponent towards them. If you have a weak open guard, you can try to keep your opponent in the closed guard (your stronger position) longer. In the event that he breaks it open, and you have to use the open guard, you can try to either bring him back to your closed guard or simply stand up and start over. It's very important, as you progress, to select which techniques work best for you. The selection should not be immediate - just because a move doesn't work right after you've learned it doesn't mean that you should give up on it - but rather, it should be slow and intelligent. As you realize that a certain technique doesn't fit your game, you should build up options that will supply similar results and substitute that technique for another, or even better, with a series of techniques. For instance, if you have trouble with the triangle, then perhaps it would be best if you concentrated on other attack options from the same position, like the armlock and the omoplata. This is much more effective than insisting on using a technique with which you're uncomfortable.

By recognizing which techniques work for you, and which don't, you will become aware of many things in your personal game. You'll be able, with more experience, to recognize that a new technique is not well suited for you, helping you to avoid wasting your precious time and energy on it so you can focus on areas that better fit your game. This knowledge will not only give you better and faster results, but will also turbo-charge your progress—your energy level and success rate will greatly improve since you're concentrating on what you can do best!

How to learn and retain information

Every time you train, you need to have an objective. The obvious objectives are to learn a new technique, improve your execution of it and better understand the game. Since Jiu-Jitsu is a very complex fighting art, there are various steps to learning. The first step is to learn a single technique. The next, is to learn counters to that technique. After that, you need to learn how to link various techniques together, transitioning between them both offensively and defensively. Understanding the requirements and objectives of the game is a step that is often overlooked. For instance, a student comes into a school and is shown a submission hold and another technique, which is often enough to send him to the sparring lines. Soon enough, the student develops a crude understanding of the game because he lacks insight or guidance from the instructor. Instead, he learns by watching other people spar. It's extremely important that, along with understanding the techniques, counters, transitions and links, you understand what each position involves – you need to know the objectives of each major position, what you need to prepare for and what you need to be thinking about in regard to each of the major positions.

Learning and retaining single techniques

Every time that you learn a single technique, whether it be an attacking technique or a counter-attack, you need to ask yourself, "Why does the move work this way? Why can't I put my hands in a certain way? Why is this wrong when it feels so natural to me?"

FIGURE 12

Your natural intuition is the worst thing that you have when beginning this art. Because Gracie Jiu-Jitsu was developed to exploit natural reaction patterns, many times you'll find that when you feel like you should pull, you should actually push. Everything you think is correct is wrong. When your instinct tells you to stiffen up, you should actually relax. For example; when you mount someone, their natural reaction is to either extend their arms and push yours off (figure 12), or to turn over. If they extend their arm, they put themselves in the perfect set up for an arm-lock from the guard. On the other hand, if they turn their backs, they give their neck up for a choke. Another example: in an arm-lock from the guard (figure 13), the person in the arm-lock will naturally want to pull away. If he does this, he straightens his arm even more and improves the lock's efficacy.

FIGURE 13

FIGURE 14

FIGURE 15

FIGURE 16

The correct action would be to put your weight forward and stack your opponent, which will help you keep your arm bent. Or let's say that you want to sweep someone to one side. In this case, you should always feign a push to the opposite side, causing him to naturally react by leaning against the push – in fact, he's actually driving his weight in the direction of the sweep.

You need to learn the whys and the whats of each move. It's also important to realize what *not* to do. When learning a new technique, don't question the move itself; simply accept the instruction (even though you might feel that it's unreasonable) and ask how the technique works and why it is effective. When you learn why you do the steps for a technique then you will never forget the technique and will always execute it properly.

If you don't have an instructor, look it up in a book – that's one of the best reasons to have a strong Jiu-Jitsu library. Just as when you were in school, you need textbooks to consult when the instructor isn't around; they give you information at your fingertips anytime and anywhere. While books can't replace a good instructor, who has a personal instructor around to consult 24 hours a day?

Learning to link and transition between techniques

Single techniques are like snap shots; they represent a moment frozen in time. Although they are dynamic, they are still only an isolated piece of the entire move. Single techniques don't occur in isolation; rather, they occur as a result of an action from your opponent during the course of a fight or sparring session. Since a single technique is part of a larger entity, it's important that you learn how to link techniques together.

There are other reasons why you need to learn how to link up techniques. First, if you're only concentrating on one attack - for instance, the choke from the mounted position (figure 14) - your opponent will use 100% of his physical and mental energy to counter it. Because defense is more effective, and requires less time to execute than attacks, his chance of successfully defending against your single attack is pretty high. In the case of a choke, all he needs for a successful defense is to block your second hand from coming in, or to turn to the side in order to prevent your second hand from grabbing the collar. If you introduce another option to the choke - in this case, the arm-lock - your opponent will have to divide his attention between two moves. Now you have created a new dimension to your attack and have forced your opponent to decide whether he will defend the choke or arm-lock. And since he's thinking under duress, his reactive intelligence will suffer, while yours, which is in control of the better position, will be sharper.

So you attack him with a choke from the mount and, upon his correct defensive reaction, you switch to the arm-lock. If he's late in defending against it, you can finish him. If, on the other hand, he somehow reacts quickly enough to defend against the arm-lock, you can go right back to the choke. With combinations, you will greatly increase your success rate in attacks and defenses. The key to an effective combination is to be able to execute the proper technique, know the possible defensive counters and when your opponent executes one of the counters, quickly transition to the appropriate counter attack choice.

FIGURE 17

It's important to initiate each technique with the full intention of succeeding with it; transition to the next option only if your opponent successfully defends against your original attack. It's also important to remember that you can go back and forth between attacks. This is because, when attacking with the second technique, your opponent will be so focused on defending the most recent attack that he may forget about the original one, allowing you to switch back and catch him off guard.

How do you learn to link moves together? The first step is to select a single technique from a position in which you excel. It doesn't matter which one - a choke from the mount (figure 14), an arm-lock from the guard, or a sweep from the open guard. Next, you need to discover the common reactions or counters to that technique. After that, organize them by their frequency. Of course, each opponent will react differently, but there's also a common thread in the way that people will respond to your attack. As an example, let's select the arm-lock from the guard and the common counter of stacking. You need to select which options are available as a response to that counter. Maybe you may have two or three options to the counter - for instance, you have the collar choke, a sweep and the triangle. Let's assume that, of the three options, you are best at executing the choke. Select that one and drill it with a partner: go from the initial arm-lock, allow your partner to counter it by stacking you and switch to the choke. Continue this until you can seamlessly transition between the two. Once you have mastered this first one-two combination you have a few choices. You can go back to the first move - in this example, the arm-lock from the guard - and look for the same stack counter, responding with their second best option (let's assume that your next best move after the choke is the sweep). Then try the same drill, but use the sweep rather than the choke. Another option is to look at the second most frequent defense option; go through the same process of studying the counters to the defense, selecting the one that you excel at and repeat the drill. Or, your last option: continue in the

FIGURE 18

FIGURE 19

process from where you stopped - in the arm-lock to choke combination - and look at the most common choke defenses with which you're faced. Find the options you have from there. Using the same logic as above, you can continue into a forward flowing link rather than a single position drill like the one before (figure 15 through 19, knee on stomach drill)

Regardless of which path you take, there are certain steps that you need to follow:

- Do not add any option to your sequence until you have the previous steps down.
- Do not add a difficult option before an easier one.
- Do not add an option that you are not good at.
- Do not add an option that rarely occurs, unless your sequence is very broad (with many options combined together).
- Always start practicing the drills with a willing partner of the same or lesser weight and size, helping you go through the sequence. After you have somewhat mastered the sequence, have your partner gradually increase the level of resistance.
- When actually employing the sequence, always go with the full intention of succeeding with every move.

How to take advantage of your biotype

You need to focus on the techniques that best fit your personal abilities, otherwise you're not only wasting valuable time, but also putting yourself in a position that may cause you to question your overall ability at Jiu-Jitsu. If you allow it, Jiu-Jitsu will mold itself to your unique body type and style. You need to allow it to adapt to you. If you or your instructor insists on focusing on the incorrect techniques for your body type, then you're straying from your path.

Let's say that you have extremely short legs. You're not going to be able to apply the triangle on large people. So instead of trying to turn the triangle into your bread and butter submission technique, you should try to perfect your choke or arm-lock. On the other hand, if you have long legs, the triangle will be a formidable weapon, so you should practice it often.

Every biotype has its strengths and its weaknesses. If you are fast, for instance, you'll be better at passing the guard loose than if you're slow. If you're slow, passing the guard tight and on the ground will most likely be better. If you are not flexible, the spider guard may be harder for you than the butterfly guard, since you are not as comfortable being stacked with your legs over your head. The important thing here is not that you realize your limitations and sulk—rather, it's that you recognize your weaknesses, learn how to avoid them when fighting, and build your game around your strengths!

Technique is power!

In Gracie Jiu-Jitsu, proper technique is based on leverage and calculations. It is based on action and reaction, not power. The Gracie Jiu-Jitsu techniques were developed to work against anyone, regardless of size or strength if you use them correctly and in the proper situation. Here's one of the most important rules that you can understand: if you are using too much power to execute a technique, you are doing it incorrectly! Techniques should work without an excessive use of power; if you are using all your energy against an opponent that is comparably strong and skilled, how are you going to handle an opponent that's bigger than you? Every time you find yourself struggling and exerting excess energy, you can be sure that you're doing something wrong. When you find yourself in this situation, you need to pause and try to understand your mistake. You should ask yourself the following questions:

- Are the mechanics of my technique wrong?
- Is my timing off?
- Am I using the proper technique for this situation?
- Am I properly setting up the technique?

Simply realizing that you're doing something wrong is a big step forward. But if you ask yourself these questions and, better yet, truthfully answer them, then you're not only solving a specific technical problem, but you're also beginning to develop a systematic way of solving your technical difficulties.

How do you go about finding the proper answers? Obviously, the first option is your instructor. When you ask him if the mechanics of a move are correct, he should be able to clarify and correct any mistakes. But while your instructor is a valuable tool, it would be even better for you to start early on by asking and answering your own questions.

Are the mechanics of my technique wrong?

Many times, if you practice a newly learned technique through training alone, skipping the repetition drills, you may slowly start to lose proper form. It doesn't happen right away. You spar frequently and make small adjustments due to specific constraints, like your partner's

size, an injury that you have or fatigue. Soon enough, your great technique is completely ineffective.

When that happens, you need to get back to the basic mechanics of the technique. The easiest way to correct this problem is to ask your instructor. If you're away from him, or if you're the most advanced person at the academy, you will have to figure it out on your own. To help you, you should go on a quest for technical books, instructional tapes and DVD's on the subject. By properly researching, you should be able to get an idea of how to correctly execute the technique. The second step is to ask your training partner. Many times, training partners realize what you're doing wrong and can easily point it out to you, putting you back in business in no time at all. The third way that you can perfect your technique is to observe someone else using the same technique. Try to figure out what you're doing differently from him.

If, after all this, you are still unsuccessful in your quest, you should break the move down and try to figure out where the problem lies. If you're having trouble with the scissor sweep (figures 20, 21 & 22), for example, you should ask: What am I having trouble with? Is it the legs, the arms or the opponent's position? Try to figure out what part of the move is not working and then, by further understanding the basics of leverage (explained later in this book) for Jiu-Jitsu, you should be able to correct your technique or, if not that, at least put yourself in the right direction.

Is my timing off?

Timing is everything in life, and this is particularly true in Gracie Jiu-Jitsu. You may be selecting the proper technique for a certain situation, but fail in your execution because you're too slow in pulling the trigger. If you find yourself in a situation in which you know that your mechanics are correct, but still fail to successfully execute the technique, then timing might be your problem. Basically, the problem is that you are seeing the moment for an attack and even selecting the right technique but *you are too slow in the execution phase*. Correct timing involves factors such as recognition, selection and execution. When you have all three of these factors working together with speed, your timing will be great!

Recognition

Recognition is the ability to see a situation develop and know how it will affect you in a fight. In order for you to even start scanning through your brain for the array of techniques that you can use in any given situation, you first need to recognize what the situation is and what opportunities and dangers it may present. To develop better recognition, you need to train often and be aware of what's happening during your sparring sessions. You can also improve your recognition by watching other people spar or compete. This is a particularly useful tool because you can calmly observe the situation far from the heat of battle.

Selection

Selection is the ability to scan through your knowledge bank for all the techniques that you know and choose the best one for the situation at hand. Selection is a difficult process that can be accelerated and optimized through linking techniques and constant drilling. This will help you create mental shortcuts for the selection process. The selection process can be tricky; it's better to slowly select the proper technique than to hastily select an improper technique for the situation.

Execution

Having properly recognized the situation, and selected the proper technique to be applied, the final step in the timing equation is execution. To improve your execution, you need to use the same methods as described above; static drills (to properly develop the neuro-mechanics of the move), situation or controlled drills (to develop the use of the technique in a dynamic environment) and sparring with a graduating scale of size and technical level, i.e. start with a light person of a lower belt and increase the size. Once you've run the entire size within that belt, go to the lightest person in the next belt and so forth.

Am I using the proper technique for this situation?

Many times, you apply what you think is the right technique for the situation, but your success rate is still low. Gracie Jiu-Jitsu is an extremely pragmatic martial art, in which success is the ultimate measuring stick. This means that if you're not having a high success rate, you may not be applying the proper technique for the situation. How do you correct that? How do you select the best technique for a situation? The answer is both complex and simple. When you're aware of the technical options and possibilities for a situation, the best technique is the one that you're most confident with and can apply with the most precision and speed, not necessarily the newest or most complicated move you know. If you have three options for a technique - an attack from the guard, for instance - the best option you can use is the one at which you excel!

So how do you learn what the options are for a situation? First, you should consult your instructor and he'll present you with a variety of options, hopefully while taking into account your technical level and

FIGURE 23

FIGURE 24

FIGURE 25

your personal abilities. If that's not sufficient, you should look at this book (and other Brazilian Jiu-Jitsu series books) and watch DVD's, observing what the masters of the sport prefer. Lastly, you can watch more advanced fighters in your academy or go to a tournament. Once you have a roadmap to follow, you need to select the techniques in order, based on the criteria above—the first option is the one that you're best at, then the second, third and so on. It's not important to have twenty options for each position; the more positions you know, the more your brain will have to search before it can select one. It's important to have at least two, and preferably three technique options for any situation.

Am I properly setting up the technique?

As you begin to learn Gracie Jiu-Jitsu, you're taught a series of techniques and they appear, on the surface, to be infallible solutions for certain situations. However, the further you progress in the sport, the more you will realize that the same technique will fail under the correct situation! The reason is that Jiu-Jitsu is a thinking man's game; your opponent may react with a counter faster than you are able to execute the initial technique. In Jiu-Jitsu, just as in all martial arts, the defense is always more powerful than the attack. While it may take two or three moves for you to set up a triangle (figures 23, 24 & 25), it takes your opponent just one to escape it (by posturing, or removing the arm, etc). This is certainly a problem—you have chosen the proper technique for the situation and you use it as quickly and perfectly as possible *but* your opponent is still escaping or countering it. In general, this is happening because you are not properly setting up the technique, which gives your opponent the extra seconds he needs to successfully react and counter. So how do you increase your success rate when applying your technique? You need to set up your opponent first. While there are too many set-ups to go over, there are some general rules which you can learn and follow that will greatly assist you.

Action-reaction

As we pointed out before, human intuition is a bad habit in Jiu-Jitsu, so use it against your opponent! Even at the highest levels - the fast changing environment, the duress and the fatigue - many people will react to a push with a push and a pull with a pull. If you want to sweep your opponent to the right, try pushing him to the left. Once he reacts by pushing to the right against you, apply your sweep in that direction. In a similar fashion, if you want your opponent to come close to you for a choke from the guard (figure 26 & 27), attempt to push him away as if you were trying to create space for an arm-lock.

Link techniques together

By using the instructions, drills and techniques that pertain to linking techniques, you will be correctly setting up your opponent. When linking the technique, it is important to attempt each technique with the full intention of succeeding with it. Otherwise, a smart opponent will sense a lack of commitment and won't react to it with the same energy.

FIGURE 26

How many techniques do I need to know to become a Black Belt?

Many times, the Gracie Jiu-Jitsu practitioner believes, or is led to believe, that he needs to know many techniques in order to achieve the coveted Black Belt. The myth exists because novices see advanced fighters using more and more sophisticated moves against one another. This is particularly true in regard to many tournament fighters, who rely on specific advanced moves to achieve success.

The young practitioner, noticing that each move has a counter and each counter has a counter to that, will assume that in order to defeat his opponent, he needs to learn the most advanced techniques he can find. It's like the quest for the Holy Grail, where the belief is that there is somehow always another technique to be learned that will be the key to his advancements.

FIGURE 27

Following that logic, and also the advice of some instructors who require a large number of techniques for belt progression, the Gracie Jiu-Jitsu practitioner will often assume that quantity is the key to success. In truth, this is hardly the case. Don't get us wrong, we're not condemning teachers simply for having a clear curriculum for belt advancement; in fact, this always helps, giving the student a clear path that he needs to seek in order to progress to the next belt level. But it is important to remember that "progress" should emphasize quality over mere quantity. It is most important to properly learn moves – to know the objectives and nuances of each technique and position – and to be able to expertly execute them.

It is much more important for a student to know how to perfectly execute, accurately select and seamlessly transition between a limited number of techniques, than to have an infinite knowledge of moves that are applied improperly.

We don't want to set a specific number of techniques that you need to learn, but we do advocate that you focus on the basics (and some variations) until you achieve a high level of technical understanding and efficiency in using them. Concentrate on quality rather than quantity. The more techniques you try to learn, the less time you'll have to properly learn each of them. Also, the greater number of techniques you know, the longer it will take for you to select the right one.

If you have 200 half-learned techniques, your brain will take a lot longer to select the appropriate one than if you have 50 sharp and mechanically solid techniques.

There is ample proof that the basics, when properly applied, will not only work, but will get you ultimate success whether it's in the academy, in a tournament fight or at a NHB tournament. Rodrigo's cousin Rickson Gracie won all his fights by submission – in everything from Jiu-Jitsu tournaments to No Holds Barred events. He won with the most basic set of moves. His legendary precision and quick-decision making made his victories appear simple—people were shocked that his opponents couldn't avoid the simplest and most basic submissions. Another of Rodrigo's cousins, Royce Gracie, won a record three UFC's in the early 90's and many other recent fights with an extremely basic game. His secret: "Do everything right!" he claims, "The fancy stuff only appears once in a while, the basics you have everyday!" Recently, another cousin, Roger Gracie, has experimented with tremendous success in the Jiu-Jitsu tournament circuit and the ADCC World Submission Wrestling, using a game that appears to be a throwback to the early years. Opponents marvel at the way he is able to maintain the mounted position and use the basic closed guard attacks on his way to World titles, which he wins mostly through submission. And again, he wins with the most basic submissions: chokes, arm-locks and chokes from the back.

You don't necessarily want to learn all the positions to the point that you can use them, but rather, you should know what they are, allowing you to recognize what the danger is and how best to neutralize it. For instance, there are many ways to pass the guard, but you only need to know two or three in order to be a top fighter. You don't need to be proficient with 20 different guard passes; just perfect the two or three that feel the most comfortable.

By following this method, you will quickly develop a solid game and be aware of the other techniques that exist (that way, you won't be surprised if they're thrown at you). Because realistically, one can't both know and be good at every position in Gracie Jiu-Jitsu— and you don't need to in order to be a good fighter and good Black Belt.

It's not the one who has the most positions that wins, but the one who chooses the right position at the right time. It's all about precision in selecting and applying the right position.

What types of techniques should I concentrate on most?

Your instructor should be your guide to the techniques that you need to learn. He's the best person to pace your progress and teach you the proper technique at the time when you're best prepared to learn and absorb it.

This book presents a series of drills and techniques that will either supplement your instructor's teaching and serve as a reference guide when you're away from the academy or, if you don't have a Black Belt instructor, it will work as a guide to be followed in order to attain your goal.

Why practitioners quit Jiu-Jitsu

There are three reasons why practitioners quit Jiu-Jitsu. They are also the three main reasons why people fail to reach Black Belt: lack of recognition or promotion, injury, and burn out.

Lack of recognition

The instructor doesn't pay enough attention to the student and fails to encourage him. The student gets no recognition or special attention from the instructor. Because of this, the student doesn't feel he is progressing and quits. The solution here is to try to speak with your instructor about your concerns, or get private lessons for more personal attention. If all else fails, change to another school where the instructor may better meet your expectations.

Injury

If you overtrain, your chances of getting injured will increase. This is because you're driving your body too hard, particularly in the beginning. When people start to train, they get enthusiastic and try to train every day, which makes it more difficult for their minds and bodies to rest properly, causing them to get injured more frequently. Another common cause of injury is from improper training, or training with an inadequate instructor. It is very important that you find an instructor who understands your goals, your body type and your level of commitment to learning Gracie Jiu-Jitsu.

Burn out

As you begin to learn Gracie Jiu-Jitsu, you'll likely fall in love with the art and want to train every day. After a period of training every day, you'll end up burning yourself out. You need to pace yourself, despite your desire to go all out and to hit the mats everyday. It's important to allow your body to gradually adjust to the rigors of training. If you don't, not only will you get burned out, but you will also increase your chances of injury (as discussed above). Gracie Jiu-Jitsu is a very involving and passionate sport. The close physical contact and the similarities to a real fight can bring out the most primal instinct in a person: survival. And when you begin to tap into that, and actually learn how to successfully use it, you'll get a tremendous dose of personal satisfaction and achievement that will drive you to train even further. It becomes an addiction of the best kind; you are physically training with passion, learning to protect yourself and learning control. You are learning how to deal with pressure, how to deal with defeat (and success), the feeling of being helpless, the feeling of having control over your actions and the feeling of having control over someone else.

Rodrigo says, "I once had a student who, when he started, got so enthused with Gracie Jiu-Jitsu that he wanted to train every day. More than that, he became so obsessed with reaching Blue Belt, that after a while, he wouldn't be satisfied with training every day—he started training two times a day! No matter how much I tried to tell him to slow down, to take a few days off and train at a more moderate pace, he wouldn't listen. He trained twice a day for a couple months when a few problems started to occur. First off, compared to the first couple weeks, his progress in the later weeks began to slow down. His mind was clogged up and he wasn't able to absorb the information. Second, he started to show signs of burning out: he was getting frustrated more often, felt that he wasn't learning and was sure that he wouldn't ever reach Blue Belt. Again, despite my efforts, he kept plowing forward and training as often as possible. Finally, he got promoted to Blue Belt, and immediately afterwards, quit! We basically never saw him again! He put so much effort into a short objective that he lost sight of the final goal—reaching Black Belt. If you want to get there, you need to train smart, pace yourself and have fun doing it! I tell my students, 'It is not a sprint, and it is not a marathon, it's a path that you enjoy following!'"

Another factor that can cause people to train too much and too hard is a relentless desire to progress and an unquenchable thirst for knowledge. Human beings always seek knowledge, and martial arts practitioners are no different. Gracie Jiu-Jitsu has been compared to playing chess with your body. The sport is centered largely on fighting intelligently, having quick mental reflexes, and being proficient with an endless number of techniques and variations. When a student first delves into the art and begins to learn the basic techniques, he begins to see how they work for him and the results of properly applying them. With this, he develops a thirst for greater knowledge. He actually begins to think that, in order to progress and reach the Black Belt, he needs to spend countless hours on the mat, fighting against the toughest opponents and learning hundreds of techniques. In reality, intelligently training and properly learning a limited number of techniques will work better for you.

If you can learn to control and diminish these detrimental factors, you are well on your way to reaching the Black Belt.

It isn't a good idea to train every day, especially at the beginning. You need to wait until you reach at least Purple Belt before you should even consider daily training. This is because, if you train every day, particularly in the beginning, sooner or later you're going to face the pitfalls of injury and burn out. If you train correctly and intelligently, you only need to train three times a week.

Everyone that starts a martial art wants to reach their goal of becoming a Black Belt. But after two or three years of training, when a person hasn't advanced, he starts to wonder, "What do I need to do to become a Black Belt? Do I need to train every day? Do I need to train hard and against the biggest guys? Do I always need to train against the best guys?" In short, the answer is no, no and no! You don't need to train every day unless you are a competitor, have a specific objective or have a short term goal, such as a tournament. You don't need to train with all the biggest guys. If you do, you will get hurt more often and that will set you back, or worse, force you to give up and quit. You certainly don't always need to train with the best guys, because if you do, you'll lose and probably start to feel discouraged. You won't be able to develop your game; instead, you'll be forced to fall back into defensive positions and focus entirely on escaping bad situations.

Instead, as we stated above, you need to train three days a week. This will allow your body and mind to rest and absorb the knowledge that you're learning at the academy. You need to train against a variety of partners, small, medium and large, which is necessary in developing your ability to deal with different body types and strengths. With the small guys, you may be able to "muscle in" some moves and escape some situations with brute force until you can figure out the proper technical execution of the move. A smaller person will be quicker, better at replacing the guard, and able to use different positions than a larger person. This will help you to develop different parts of your game. For the same reason, you also need to train with a variety of partners with different skills. When you train with the talented guys, you will learn through observation and experience how to do their moves; you will feel their weight distribution, their pressure and the way that they defend certain attacks. You'll absorb the techniques without even noticing. But the drawback is that, most of the time, you aren't in control of the training and usually can't use the technique that you want. When you train against a less skilled opponent, you'll be able to control the training and be able to repeat the technique that you're learning with greater frequency. This will allow you to develop the nuances that will make a position work for you.

How to best teach your student

This section is meant for primarily for instructors, but students can also learn much about how instructors teach.

Jiu-Jitsu is like mathematics; there are precise principles of the art that hold true in any fight. For instance, if your opponent is putting his weight back, and you're trying to pull him forward, it will be difficult for you to achieve the desired result. It makes a lot more sense to realize that, because his weight is back, you should select a move that exploits it. Another important thing to remember is that the more power you use while learning or training, the longer it's going to take for you to fully learn a new technique. That's one of the reasons that kids are more likely to learn a technique properly; they aren't strong enough to force a technique through; rather, in order to make it effective, they have to learn the technique precisely. Once they grow older, they can add power to their already perfected mechanics.

If you're strong, and you like to use power all the time, you may be able to power your way through moves. But while you might have success most of the time, when you're forced to fight against someone stronger or heavier and you're tired, you can't rely on your strength. Your techniques will fail. For that reason, if you're a really strong person and usually find yourself using your strength during training, we recommend that you come to the academy after you've had a long workout. This way, you're already tired when you arrive and can't use 100% of your power. Oftentimes, Rodrigo puts his students through physical training before he shows them a new technique. He can do that in several different ways; he can have them do warm up exercises and other drills until he sees that they're tired, or he may wait until the very end of the class. After they've finished sparring, he introduces a new technique and has them practice and drill it repeatedly. Rodrigo makes sure that they are tired enough that they have to correctly learn the mechanics of the technique, without using their power.

Training your mind is just as important as training your body. If you introduce too many techniques when the mind is overtaxed and struggling to synthesize all the information it has already learned, you're just adding confusion and more difficulty to an already difficult situation. That's why students often go through pits and valleys, and this is particularly true for new students. At first, when he only has to decide between a handful of situations, the mental process is simple and quick: "I can only do A, B, C & D!"

Four choices are much easier to select from than 15, 30 or 100. And while the four choices may not be the best answer to every situation, they are the only options that the student has, which helps him to develop a neuro-mechanical reaction pattern, increasing his speed and efficiency.

The moment an instructor introduces too many new things, he creates chaos and sets back his student's progress. Many of you have been to a seminar where the instructor bedazzled you with twenty new positions, but then, upon leaving, you realize that you don't even remember two of them. And if you can hardly remember the techniques, imagine trying to properly remember the mechanics and knowing when best to apply them. It's a system overload! If you're taught a complex technique that's too advanced for your level, most of the time you'll never learn the way to reach the position for the technique to work, particularly if you're sparring with people of a similar (or better) level. Furthermore, you're not going to be able to see or know how to do the moves. It's like teaching a newborn to ride a bicycle: the baby is simply not mature enough, let alone close to the situation when he might be able to use the information. Rodrigo: "At times, a student will come to me with a new position he learned somewhere else and ask me to show him how to improve it. My reply to him is that, instead of trying to learn a technique that is too complex, he should concern himself with correcting the many errors and weaknesses that he already has in his game. If you focus on improving the moves that you already know, you will not only have faster results, but you will also solidify the base of your game and form a great foundation for later progression."

Learning new positions has to happen at the right time. In order to speed up the process and have a student learn with greater speed, an instructor has to emphasize the basics and encourage the student to improve what he's naturally drawn to. For instance, if a student naturally likes to pass the guard while standing, he should be given details and tips on how to improve the move. The student can ask for the principles of the standing guard pass which will allow him to improve on something that he already likes, rather than forcing him to pass the guard low and on the ground (where he doesn't feel comfortable). Remember: the quickest way for a student to improve is to work on his natural tendencies, rather than to force himself to change everything.

The next step is to learn to link up moves. When a student first learns and masters a certain move or moves, he will have more success with some than others. Once he finds a move that catches people, he'll begin to use it often. After a while, everyone will figure out

FIGURE 28

FIGURE 29

what he likes to do; they'll start to anticipate the move and defend against it more effectively. It's no surprise that when this happens, the student's success rate will go down.

A teacher needs to teach the student the next option that's available from his point of difficulty. Take the example of a student who is good with the kimura (figure 28). At first, he catches everyone with it during training. But after some time, everyone already knows that he is going to try to get the kimura and they not only avoid the move, but also get good at defending against it. When he approaches his instructor, thinking that the kimura is no longer working, the instructor needs to show him the options and alternatives that he can use to build on top of the kimura. Since everyone can defend against his kimura, he needs to be ready to change his strategy, depending on how his opponents defend and react. Instead of leaving him at a dead end, forcing him to eventually abandon a good position that he executes well, an instructor can open up a few more avenues for him to explore. He not only doesn't lose what he already has, but he'll actually become more effective with it.

Rodrigo: "One time, I was training with a student who was very good at the omoplata (figure 29). And I'd let him catch the finish, I would defend it every time and we would just be stalemated there. At the end of the training, I told him, 'Your omoplata is very good, but you don't have any options once I defend against it. How do you think I'm defending it?' And he didn't know the answer. I told him, 'I'm using my arms to block your legs. You need to force me so that my arms aren't free to defend. So what you need to do is to try to break my balance. That will force me to use my arms as a brace in order to block you and prevent your sweep. At that point, my arms are busy avoiding one thing so they can't, at the same time, be free to counter your omoplata. Now you've solved the problem!' In the process, you create continuity, giving him options to move from on position to another, rather than leaving him completely unconnected."

It's also very important that, when expanding the horizons in a continuous manner, an instructor makes sure that the student understands that he should try to succeed with the first option, only moving to another appropriate option once that one fails. Unless he goes for each technique with the intention of succeeding with it, the opponent will sense a lack of commitment and won't worry enough to fully defend against it. This will cause the next move in the sequence to be less useful.

If an instructor forces a student to work on the moves that the instructor likes, then they will need the same body characteristics. And that's usually not the case. For instance, a weaker person should emphasize chokes and triangles (figure 30), because they're more technical moves and require less power than something like the arm-locks (figure 31).

FIGURE 30

The ideal student is the one who comes in the door with a good attitude and an open mind. If he's interested in learning, he's going to become a skilled fighter. This may seem simple - one might think that everyone who comes into the academy eager to learn, but this is not always the case and a good instructor will recognize this. At times, you have some people who will come in with a closed mind and a preconceived idea about the martial art, and when the art doesn't immediately meet their expectations, they turn sour and quit. Other times, a student will have a certain timetable for his progress that is completely unrealistic. Or, they just have unrealistic expectations—they think that they'll be able to defeat anyone any after six months of training. It is up to the instructor to foster a good attitude and help set reasonable goals. The best student is the one that comes without a closed mind, ready to learn and to listen to instructions. He will listen to what he is told, absorb it, adapt it to his own body and characteristics, and come back for corrections and advice. Anyone with this attitude, anyone who wants to learn and believes in his instructor, will progress.

FIGURE 31

In reality, you should at most teach two techniques a day. A good sequence is to teach a position, have the students drill it, and then have them spar with other students for a while. At the end of class, once they're tired, have them repeat the position several times with a partner. This is because, once they're tired, they can't use power; they have to rely on proper mechanics. The brain works in such a way that, when you're really tired and repeat the moves with the proper mechanics, you'll absorb it and forever remember how to do the technique correctly.

Another key to speed up the process in your path to the Black Belt is to drill the moves over and over. Professional and Olympic athletes repeat the same move several times. Take basketball players. Just think how many times they drill passing and shooting in comparison to actually playing the game. Normally they drill passing and shooting, then scrimmage while focusing on specific plays and drills. After that, they usually play a short game to see how things work and then, once practice is over, the best guys will go off and drill the moves more on their own. In any sport, drilling and repetition is much more important than actually playing the game. Unfortunately, in Jiu-Jitsu, people tend to do the opposite—they spar because it is fun, but hardly ever do the repetition of the techniques.

It's up to the instructor to pace students' progress but students also have to learn to pace themselves. Instructors should narrow down options so students will learn the basics and principles of each position and technique before they try to expand their repertoire too much. That's another reason why beginners get hurt; they spar before they're ready and end up in positions that they don't fully understand. When this happens they'll either execute the move incorrectly or remain unaware of the impending lock until it's too late and it hurts before they can submit or say "Stop." The beginning student should focus more on the repetition of techniques than on sparring, particularly when beginning to work on a new move. The new student should do repetition and controlled drills, and, if they spar, they should be properly matched with a more advanced student and limit the match to 5 minutes. This should go on for the first 4 to 6 months (it can be shortened or lengthened depending on the individual). The goal is to have the individual understand what sparring is and give him time for his body to adapt to the rigors of training.

Of course, depending on the person's background, the progress will be different. If they have done judo, wrestling or Sambo, they will already be familiar with training and their mind will be prepared for grappling. From a karate and kick-boxing background, they will likely be thinking about how they would punch from any given situation, which might distract in the beginning from focusing on the instructions. Eventually, they will start to forget about striking and begin to focus more on grappling. In many cases, when learning Gracie Jiu-Jitsu, it's better to not have any martial art experience than to have experience with a striking art; a person inexperienced with striking arts will focus solely on the grappling and not think about striking. People with past experiences in other martial arts will always try to bring this old knowledge into their new fighting repertoire.

Lots of students, and sometimes even the instructors, ask themselves, "What do I need to do to get to the next Belt?" And many times, their answer is to train with higher belts until they can hold their own. What is needed is a clear direction as to what the student needs in order to achieve the next level and it is up to the instructor to provide that direction.

Training with a Gi versus No-Gi training

Rodrigo feels that it's extremely important to train with a gi, especially in the beginning phases of learning. "If you begin Gracie Jiu-Jitsu and start immediately training without the gi, or never train with it, your guard passes and your defenses will be poor. If you want to have a technical guard and be better technically overall, you need to train with it. When I say that it's important to always train with a gi, I don't mean that you should never train without it."

In the beginning, when you train with the gi, you have many more options of attacks and controls, helping you to learn the proper defensive and posture habits. Furthermore, you are forced to use your hip movement a lot more because your opponent can hold on to your gi pants.

In addition to increasing options of control and attack, the gi adds an element of traction. This forces you to be more aware of the perfect postures and the perfect ways to move and also forces you to develop your ability to recognize and defend attacks. When you train without the gi, you are more slippery and things are a lot less precise. Without the gi, the emphasis is on speed and recovery, while with the gi, emphasis is in precision and awareness.

That is not to say that you should never train without the gi. There are times, due to a specific goal, that you should train without the gi. Rodrigo trains without a gi when he has a fight coming up, or if he is getting read to enter into a Submission Wrestling tournament like the ADCC, which he won in '98. In this case, he would train strictly without a gi for a certain amount of time before the event. But other than that, he generally prefers to train with it.

Even if you don't have a specific objective, such as fighting or a Submission Wrestling tournament, you still have much to gain from training without the gi. Without it, you develop speed and recovery, and your body adjusts and retains positions. But for anyone interested in becoming a top Jiu-Jitsu fighter, and especially achieving a Black Belt, you have to train with the gi. For the beginner, the first six months are crucial; you need to train exclusively with the gi during this time. As you progress in your training, you should still continue to predominately train with the gi.

Advancing in the Gracie Jiu-Jitsu Belt system

White through Purple Belt is the most important period of time for a student; they are developing their personal style. Some people are able to change after they reach Brown Belt, but 85% of the practitioners have set their style by the time they're Purple Belts. A Black Belt today is doing the same moves that he was doing as a Purple Belt, except that he executes them faster and more effectively.

In order to turbo-charge your progress during that phase (White to Purple), you need to get a partner, practice drills and repeat techniques often. A great way to quickly improve is to look at your body type and find a top fighter with a similar one. Examine what they do; what moves they use, how they apply them and how the application differs against different opponents. To do this, you need to attend competitions and watch DVD's of top tournaments, always closely examining the different styles.

FIGURE 32

FIGURE 33

What does the White Belt need in order to achieve Blue Belt?

The White Belt usually quits after six months because he doesn't understand Gracie Jiu-Jitsu and thinks the art is not for him. It's important for the White Belt to realize that Jiu-Jitsu is an art that's vastly more complex than most other martial arts; he needs to embrace this and learn the techniques that are presented to him. The White Belt should learn the techniques and drill them as much as possible without trying to focus on the entire game. He should focus on them, not the future. The White Belt should, as much as possible, watch the more advanced belts spar. He should try to learn from what they do without becoming enamored with the advanced techniques that they use.

Sometimes, a White Belt will watch a complex move and, because it looks fancy, immediately want to learn it for himself. In reality, the move is inappropriate for him; he hasn't matured enough in the art to properly learn and execute it. The White Belt needs to learn and practice the basics, over and over again, until he has them down.

The White Belt's classes should generally be one hour long and should be basic positions and repetition drills. He can't be thrown into a full sparring situation; he's not ready in any way, shape or form to do that. He doesn't even know what the danger is, or how to protect himself in training. The White Belt should be shown lots of basic and self-defense techniques, which are practical and might help him right away if he falls into a bad situation. It's not good to teach him advanced techniques that involve multiple steps because it won't help him—he'll feel as though it's useless, impossible to accomplish and will eventually want to quit.

Blue Belt quits before the Purple because of lack of motivation

Having achieved the Blue Belt, the Jiu-Jitsu practitioner sets his sights on his next goal—the Purple Belt. But getting there is not easy and the process is extremely slow. It isn't uncommon for someone to spend three or four years as a Blue Belt until they reach Purple, and after that, go from Purple to Black in under four years. The Purple Belt is the hardest belt to achieve and many times the student quits at this level because of lack of motivation. When you reach this level, your game is already developed; you have a full understanding of the art, can combine multiple techniques together and have a pretty good sense of which techniques are best for which situation.

The Blue Belt needs to focus on understanding the game and linking techniques. At the Purple level and above, attacks with a single technique will not yield the same results. As the practitioner's awareness increases, it becomes harder and harder to succeed without combinations of attacks and defenses.

The Blue Belt can start to learn how to set up the techniques and link these techniques together. For instance, if you go for the arm-lock from the guard and your opponent escapes, you would change to the triangle (figures 32 through 35). This is the phase where you'll start to understand movement and begin to link techniques together.

Purple Belt on his way to Brown quits because of injury
Once he has achieved Purple Belt, the Gracie Jiu-Jitsu practitioner has reached an elite status. At this point, he knows that he belongs in the art, loves it and thinks about it all the time. The Purple Belt is a great belt because, in it, you'll learn all the moves that you need to progress and can spar against almost anyone in the academy without feeling overmatched. The Purple Belt links more and more techniques together and increases the speed between each move. This belt is also the time to develop your defensive skills. At this level, it's recommended that, at times of sparring, you allow your opponent to reach an advantage - or even a dangerous position - so you can practice fighting in a tough situation, maintaining your calm and your wits, and escaping the trouble while avoiding the submission. The proper process to this is to follow a proficiency ladder; begin with the lightest and lowest belt level, increase the opponent's weight, and once you finish the heaviest in that belt, progress to the next belt, starting with the lightest weight, and so on.

The difference between the Purple Belt and the Brown and Black Belts is that the Brown Belt - and more so with the Black Belt - is capable of executing the same techniques quickly and more accurately. His mental decisions are sharper, faster and better than the Purple Belt. Many people realize at a higher level that they do the same things they did at Purple Belt, except that they do it better. Many times a Purple Belt, when sparring against an advanced belt, appears to be fighting on equal levels—the difference is in timing and the quality of the decisions. One of the main reasons a person will quit after the Purple Belt is because of injury. Upon reaching the Purple Belt, the practitioner is so eager to progress further up the belt ladder that he may overtrain and get injured. So make sure that you check out the part in this book on over-training and practice at a sensible rate that allows your body the rest it needs.

The Brown Belt
The Brown Belt is perhaps the most fun and best belt in the Jiu-Jitsu belt system. The Brown Belt has all the knowledge and most of the technical execution of a Black Belt, except he lacks the added responsibility that the Black Belt carries. The Brown Belt walks around the

FIGURE 34

FIGURE 35

academy with pride of being one step away from the ultimate goal without having to be perfect; he always has a cushion when performing before others because, after all, he's not a Black Belt yet! Brown and Black Belts have the same game that they had as Purple Belts, but they are better and quicker at making decisions, and are able to see and set up moves that are three, four or five moves ahead. The Brown Belt is the pre-graduation to the Black Belt.

To reach the highest level, the Brown Belt needs to refine his technical skills, sharpen his timing and improve his ability to select moves. Time on the mat, training and asking his instructor how best to execute his techniques are the keys at this level.

What you need to know to be a Black Belt

The Black Belt is the person who knows everything in Jiu-Jitsu; he needs to learn and know self-defense techniques, the sports aspects of the Jiu-Jitsu and the street fighting parts as well. The Jiu-Jitsu that was taught to Grandmasters Carlos and Helio Gracie was not a competition/tournament style of Jiu-Jitsu, it was a martial art created for self-defense and survival against street aggression. Carlos and Helio perfected it by using the art against different fighters in real fight situations, allowing them to refine the techniques, keeping only the ones that really worked. Carlos took an ad in a local newspaper with an open challenge to anyone who wanted to test themselves against him and his brothers. Helio had many well-documented battles against top fighters from around the world. Over the years, the Gracie family has fought many battles in various arenas, constantly developing the art and making sure that the efficiency of the techniques keep up with the changing times.

As the art progressed and expanded its reach in society by adding more practitioners, tournaments started to pop up everywhere and the sports aspect of the art became dominant. Nowadays, lots of athletes are very successful in the sports portion and know nothing about self-defense and street fighting. If you don't know self-defense, you can't be a Gracie Jiu-Jitsu Black Belt! It won't matter how many fancy sweeps you know if a street fighter gets you in a headlock and won't let you escape. And the Gracie Jiu-Jitsu Black Belt should be able to defend himself from a common street attack.

To be a Black Belt, you need to know both the basics of the art and the self-defense aspect. You don't need to be a champion competitor to achieve the top ranking. That's not to say that competition doesn't have its merits. It generally demonstrates a level of efficiency in using the techniques against opponents. Competition is the closest thing to an all-out fight, minus the strikes and the intent to hurt. It also helps you develop emotional control. But, as stated before, competition has its drawbacks. First, the rules and the specialty moves have at times skewed the fight towards a very specific style that is far from the street style. Second, tournament matches begin under a controlled situation with a referee telling you that the fight is about to start – on the streets an aggressor may surprise you.

The Black Belt should also know how to teach. Teaching is one of the best things that one can do to fully learn the intricacies and nuances of Jiu-Jitsu. For this reason, it is encouraged that, with your instructor's permission and supervision, you assist teaching classes starting at the Brown Belt level (sometimes, depending on your instructor and his confidence in your skills, he may want you to begin this at Purple Belt).

What teaching does for you cannot be overestimated. You will have to create a process of resolving technical problems for a variety of people. When you teach you have to put yourself in other people's shoes and figure out their difficulty - why a technique doesn't work for them and how you can make it work. That forces you to fully analyze and understand the techniques and principles behind it. By doing this, you will further expand your own knowledge, and even your ability to solve your own problems without help from an instructor (although at times, you may need to consult with a more advanced instructor).

Training with different people
Training with different people is one of the best ways to quickly develop your Jiu-Jitsu skills. People of differing size, weight and technical skills will make you a well-rounded fighter. Smaller and lighter people are generally quicker than you and they force you to develop your agility, thinking and reactive speed. They also are better at replacing the guard and find ways to sneak out of positions, which will force you to have a very tight game.

Bigger and heavier people are generally slower than you, giving you more time to think and select a technique. On the other hand, they have more power than you, which will force you to use proper technique in order to succeed. Because of their size, they generally have a tougher time replacing the guard and allow more space for you to replace the guard. In this sense, larger people allow you to work both ends of the guard game: passing and defending.

Fighters with lesser technical skills allow you to work on your offensive ability. Since you can partially control the sparring session, you can focus on certain areas of your game and even try new techniques until you have honed them enough to be used against more skilled fighters.

FIGURE 36

Fighters with greater technical skills than you generally force you to work on your defensive abilities. As they're better than you, you'll find yourself in difficult situations more frequently, forcing you to learn to control your emotions and to use your best defensive skills. Note that you can work on your defensive skills with a lesser technical fighter as well, by allowing them to achieve a "good" position on you. You may even allow them to start the session, or the controlled sparring, in an advantageous situation - such as having your back with hooks on (figure 36) - and work on your escapes.

Training and progress in the Academy: Don't get discouraged

You don't have to train hard every day. If you're an athlete in a different sport and are totally fit, you might be able to train every day, but the regular student, who works during the day and attends the academy at night, may not be fit enough to stand the rigors of everyday training. There must be different standards for different people with different backgrounds; if you're a 50-year old accountant, you can't compare yourself to a 20-year old marine! You just can't expect the same output of power and stamina, but, on the other hand, you can expect to learn techniques at a high level and gain the ability to defend and control a situation. So just because the 20-year old marine might be tougher than a 50-year old accountant, doesn't mean that the accountant shouldn't be promoted—he'll be progressing in technical knowledge and efficiency, and while it may not show against other trained partners at the academy, it would definitely show against a regular person.

It's very important to realize and remember that everyone at the academy trains and (for the most part) progresses together. This means that at times you might not feel like you're progressing at all; if you don't feel like you're fighting more effectively against your partner, it's probably because he's progressed too. But against an untrained person, you're progressing immensely. The problem is the reference point. Because your partners are training with you, you don't notice the relative progress, but when you're faced with an outside opponent, or with an opponent who's not regularly training, you'll be amazed and think, "Whoa! I really can control this person!"

It's very important to remember that Gracie Jiu-Jitsu is so efficient that a person, even after very few lessons, can start to apply the techniques in an effective way. That has its good points - because a new student learns techniques that are useful right away in self-defense situations – but it also has some bad points; if you've been training for a long time and come up against someone who is strong and has been training for a month, he might be able to give you a hard time and make you doubt your own abilities. It's at this moment that you need to not get discouraged and remember how effective the art is even at an early stage. Remember, in relation to a layperson outside of the Jiu-Jitsu world, you're progressing very quickly.

MEET THE TEAM

AUTHORS

Rodrigo Gracie

Rodrigo Gracie is the young lion of the Gracie clan, an international sensation since he burst on the scene in 2002 with a stunning victory in Pride, the most important event in the Ultimate Fighting world. The grandson of Brazilian Jiu-Jitsu founder Carlos Gracie, Rodrigo now has a string of victories at Pride and is one of the major draws there, fighting before tens of thousands of spectators. With a winning record and with unlimited potential, Rodrigo is fast becoming the next superstar of Brazilian Jiu-Jitsu. Despite his prowess in the NHG arena, Rodrigo's greatest strength is his ability to teach and convey to his students the essence of Gracie Jiu-Jitsu. He is in high demand for seminars around the World and his own academy in Los Angeles is busy with celebrities and regular students looking to learn from one of the best ever.

Rodrigo can be contacted by email at rodrigo@roycegracie.com

Kid Peligro

One of the leading martial arts writers in the world, Kid Peligro is responsible for regular columns in *Throwdown* and *Gracie Magazine*, as well as one of the most widely read Internet MMA news page, *ADCC News*. He has been the author or coauthor of an unprecedented string of bestsellers in recent years, including *The Gracie Way, Brazilian Jiu-Jitsu: Theory and Technique, Brazilian Jiu-Jitsu Self-Defense Techniques, Brazilian Jiu-Jitsu Black Belt Techniques, Brazilian Jiu-Jitsu Submission Grappling Techniques*, and *The Essential Guard*. A Black Belt in Jiu-Jitsu who trains with the world's best, Kid is considered to be on the cutting edge of technical knowledge. His broad involvement in the martial arts has led him to travel to the four corners of the Earth as an ambassador for the sport that changed his life. He makes his home in San Diego.

ASSISTANTS

Shawn Williams

Shawn Williams has been training Brazilian Jiu-Jitsu for the past nine years, achieving the rank of Black Belt. Williams was awarded his Black Belt by Renzo Gracie and was one of the head instructors at that academy before moving to the West Coast to follow his dream of opening his own academy: Hollywood Brazilian Jiu-Jitsu. Besides being an excellent instructor Shawn is a great competitor with such titles as four time NAGA Champion, two time Grapplers Quest Champion and International Pro-Am Champion.

In addition to teaching full time at his academy, Shawn helps Rodrigo prepare for his fights as the leading sparring partner and coach for the groundwork. Because of his wide involvement in the various aspects of fighting, Shawn stays close to the cutting edge of Brazilian Jiu-Jitsu and is one of Rodrigo's most trusted advisors and personal friend.

Shawn can be reached at:
Hollywood Brazilian Jiu-Jitsu
1106 N. La Cienega Blvd #103
W. Hollywood, CA 90069
310.360.0544
email: shawn@hollywoodbjj.com

Travis Gordon

Travis Gordon is Rodrigo's conditioning trainer and advisor. Travis is a 10-year veteran as an Exercise Therapist. Starting his career at age 17 with a high school internship, Travis has taken the opportunity to place himself in a position to learn from numerous people. He learned a wealth of nutritional education from Quantum Nutrition Labs of Torrance, CA; gained a discipline in Shiatsu Massage from the Shiatsu Massage School of California in Santa Monica, CA; and finally reached the pinnacle of his education at the National College of Exercise Professionals (NCEP) in Redondo Beach, CA.

Travis currently resides in Redondo Beach and works as a Sport Exercise Therapist and as the NCEP' s Operations Manager and one of its Senior Instructors.

He can be contacted at NCEPtraining@verizon.net

DRILLS

Drills are the most effective way to train your mind and body to execute a move without thinking. Because positions and situations occur very rapidly both in competition and on the street, if you have to think before you execute, your decisions will come too late to help you. Drilling trains your body and mind to react almost instinctively to the situations that are developing in front of you. You want to get reactive to the point that it comes out automatically, just as when someone throws something in your face, you immediately blink your eyes and put your hands up to protect the face.

Remember that at the higher levels of Gracie Jiu-Jitsu it is not the number of techniques that one knows that makes the difference. The difference comes with timing, timing being defined as selecting and executing the proper technique for the situation.

Be sure to practice these drills to both sides of your body in equal numbers of repetitions so you can be at skilled at executing the moves on either side. We recommend practicing each drill at least ten times from each side, either alternating sides with each repetition, or working on one side at a time.

BASIC DRILLS

1

Hip escape

The hip escape is one of the most important movements in Gracie Jiu-Jitsu. The hip escape is commonly thought of as a way of escaping from the side-control and the mounted position, but it is useful for much more than that. It is the basis for creating space and adjusting the position of your hips in relation to your opponent's hips. Just about every submission or sweep attempt and most of the guard adjustments involve the hip escape. One of the most important things that the hip escape accomplishes is to turn your body to the side so your back is not flat on the ground, allowing the body to move more freely. Anytime you have your back on the ground you are easily pinned and your escape movements are hindered. Practice this drill frequently, especially prior to your training session. Use it as a warm up to not only get your hips and legs loosened up but also as a way to improve your ground movement.

1 Rodrigo lies flat on his back with his legs extended and arms at his side.

2 He coils his right leg so that his heel is as close to his buttocks as possible.

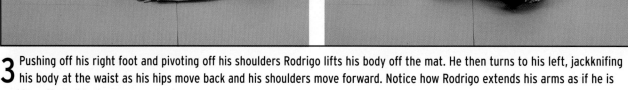

3 Pushing off his right foot and pivoting off his shoulders Rodrigo lifts his body off the mat. He then turns to his left, jackknifing his body at the waist as his hips move back and his shoulders move forward. Notice how Rodrigo extends his arms as if he is pushing off an object or an opponent.

Front View

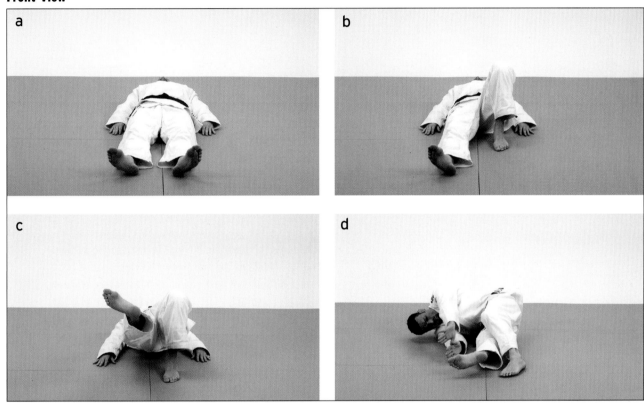

Notice how Rodrigo lifts his entire body off the ground while keeping his body straight. This is very important – he creates space for an escape from a difficult position. If you don't raise the hips and the body off the ground your opponent may be able to keep you flat and prevent you from escaping the hips out while turning to one side. Notice that the movement is like a pike or jackknife position, with the hips moving back and away from the center line.

2

Turning to your knees, or turtle position

Turning to your knees is another basic and very important movement in Gracie Jiu-Jitsu. It is used in many situations, such as escape from side-control, or as a way to prevent a guard pass.

Although the movement seems very simple, there are ways to make it more effective, as Rodrigo demonstrates here.

1 Rodrigo lies on his back with his legs coiled and the feet close to his hips.

2 Pushing off his feet and pivoting off his shoulders, Rodrigo raises his hips off the ground.

a

3 Here is the key to effectively executing the move: Instead of switching the legs in a scissoring motion Rodrigo maintains the pressure of his right foot as he swings his left foot back and under his right leg while he turns his torso to his left. Maintaining pressure with the right foot and swinging the left leg under keeps Rodrigo's hips from being pushed down flat by an opponent. If he used the scissoring motion Rodrigo wouldn't have any leg contact with the ground. Rodrigo turns to his knees with his torso facing down.

b

c

3

Turning to your knees alternative (scissoring the legs)

At times your opponent allows you the freedom to turn your body over without pressuring you down. In that case scissoring the legs will work as a faster way to turn to your knees. It is important to generate momentum much like a break dancer does, using your legs to help your motion.

1 Rodrigo starts to turn to his stomach. He pushes off his right foot while turning his body to his left.

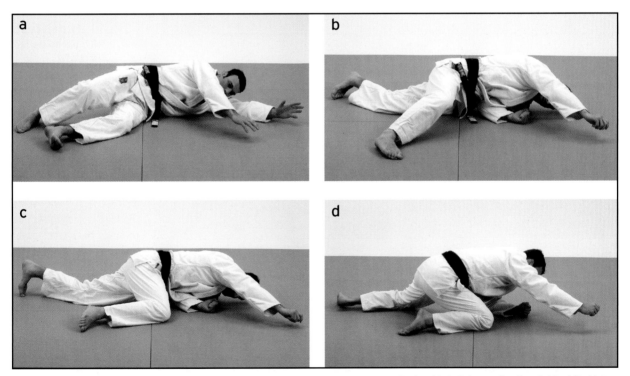

2 Using one quick motion to generate momentum, Rodrigo scissors his legs, bringing his left leg under the right while kicking the right leg over. This motion twists his body to the left. Rodrigo turns to his knees. Notice that during the drill Rodrigo reaches with his right arm as if grabbing onto his opponent's body.

4

Forward and backward shoulder roll

Being able to roll forward and backwards is of great importance in both sports and self-defense Jiu-Jitsu. The roll is not only useful in situations like replacing the guard and other technical aspects, but also as a way to break a fall. One cannot overestimate the importance of properly learning to fall, so Rodrigo goes into great detail in this and the next few drills to teach the proper technique. It is always important to learn to crawl before you can walk or run; in the early stages of learning to roll you should start on your knees. Slowly raise the difficulty level by having your torso further from the ground until you are able to execute the move from the standing position.

1 Rodrigo starts on all fours with his legs bent, knees and hands touching the mat.

a

b

c

d

2 Rodrigo opens his right arm and leans forward so the right shoulder touches the mat. At the same time he turns his head away from the shoulder that he is going to roll over (the right). Pushing off his toes, Rodrigo rolls over the right shoulder and lands sitting on the mat. It is important to roll *over the shoulder and not the head* otherwise you may compromise your neck and spine. This is especially important in a street situation where you may be rolling to soften a fall or a takedown. Rolling over the head will not only be bad for the neck and spine but you will have no cushioning in case the ground is not smooth and may be covered with rocks or other debris.

3 To roll backwards Rodrigo repeats the motion in reverse. Pushing off his feet, Rodrigo sits back, extends the right arm out while throwing his legs over the right shoulder, ending up on all fours in the same manner he started the rolling drill. Notice that in both rolling forward and back Rodrigo uses the opposite hand (in this case the left) to assist in the push and the balance as he rolls over the right shoulder.

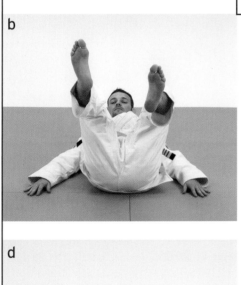

Break fall drill 1: Sitting

The next step in drilling falling and rolling is learning to use the arms. In this case Rodrigo slams the forearms on the ground as a way to defuse the impact of the fall as he rolls back. If Rodrigo had been tripped or was thrown back, his arms would take away the major part of the impact and soften the fall.

1 Rodrigo sits on the mat with the legs semi-flexed and the heels touching the mat. His arms are straight and parallel to the mat.

2 Pushing back off his feet, Rodrigo rolls backwards as he opens his arms. He slams the forearms on the mat, lessening the impact of the fall on his back. Notice that Rodrigo opens his arms slightly wider than the knees in order to clear the knees and to have the most effect in absorbing the impact.

Side View:

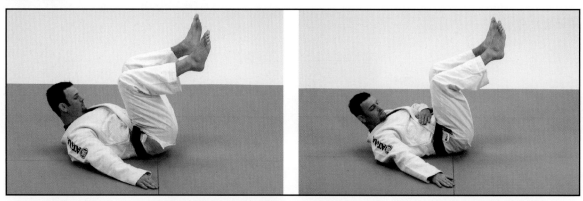

You can do the drill with both arms open simulating falling straight back or with one arm open and the other bent touching the stomach, simulating a fall to the side.

Break fall drill 2: Kneeling

The next step in the falling drills is to start from a kneeling position.

1 Rodrigo begins the drill with his right leg forward, bent at the knee, while kneeling down on his left knee. His arms are straight out and parallel to the ground, his head up with the eyes looking forward. Notice that his left leg is angled in with the foot past the line with the right foot.

2 Rodrigo pushes back off his right foot and he brings the left leg forward so he can sit on the mat as he falls back. Rodrigo opens his arms and slams the forearms on the mat to absorb the impact of the fall.

7

Break fall drill 3: Crouching

Once you have mastered falling from the kneeling position start from standing on your toes in a crouch.

1 Rodrigo starts in a crouch on the tip of his toes with the arms out before him.

2 Pushing off the toes, Rodrigo falls back while using the forearms to hit the mat first to break the impact of the fall.

8

Break fall drill 4: Side to side

Since you don't know which way you are going to be thrown, it is very important to learn to break the fall to either side. Rodrigo demonstrates a drill to assist you in developing that movement.

1 Rodrigo lies on his back with his legs and arms pointing up. The legs are semi-flexed.

2 Rodrigo falls to his left. As he rolls to his left, he uses the right foot and left arm to slam into the mat to reduce the impact of the fall. Notice that the right foot with the right leg bent at the knee and the left arm hit the ground before the left leg touches the mat. Notice that Rodrigo's right arm is bent with the hand touching the stomach. The left leg can be slightly more extended than the right one. Rodrigo returns to center and repeats the motion to the right side, using the opposite limbs to take the impact, the left leg and right arm hit the mat first.

9

Break fall drill 5: Standing

The next step in learning to properly fall is to start the motion from a standing position. At this point you should have mastered the previous drills and are perfectly adept at falling from the crouch position.

1 Rodrigo begins the drill standing with the feet shoulder width apart. He steps forward diagonally with the left leg until the foot is past his right foot and swings his left arm across his body to the right at the same time he starts to rotate his body to the right. Notice that Rodrigo's arm is straight.

2 Rodrigo flexes his right leg, lowering his body towards the mat as his left leg and arm continue the swing towards the right. At this point the leg and arm swing have forced Rodrigo's body to turn towards the right. This is important because as Rodrigo falls to the ground he wants to hit with the left side of the body and not with his back. This way his muscles and not the spine will absorb the impact of the fall. Also notice that Rodrigo doesn't just fall back – he lowers his body by bending the right leg until he is low enough to the ground. The limb movement makes his body fall to the mat. Rodrigo hits the mat with his left arm first to defuse the full impact of the fall. His right arm is bent at the elbow with the palm of the hand touching his stomach. Rodrigo's left leg clears the right and hits the ground sideways as well.

Incorrect:
Notice that Rodrigo's legs come down together, with the right one on top of the left. This causes the knees to hit together and may cause injury. Make sure your bottom leg clears the other so your knees don't hit.

10

Break fall drill 6: Partner hip throw

Once you have mastered falling on your own it is time to step up and put it to use. Partner up with a friend and have him execute a hip throw on you. The hip throw is a great throw to practice in order to learn the art of falling because of the great amplitude of the throw and because your partner can (and should!) control your fall.

1 Shawn applies a hip throw on Rodrigo. With Rodrigo standing behind him, Shawn grabs Rodrigo's right arm with his hands and pulls Rodrigo over his back while locking the right hip in front of Rodrigo's hips.

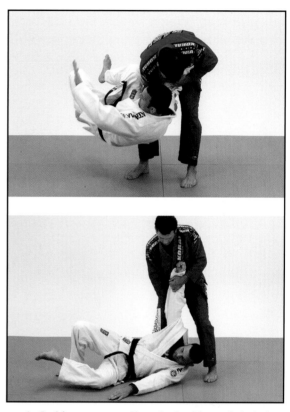

2 As Rodrigo goes over Shawn's shoulder and starts to free fall, he turns his body so that the left side is facing down and prepares to break the fall with his left arm extended and right leg bent, both ready to hit the mat before his body does. Shawn controls the fall by holding onto and pulling up Rodrigo's right arm.

Incorrect A:

Rodrigo falls flat on the ground. This is a grave mistake. His head and spine hit the ground without any cushioning and may cause serious injuries. Make sure to *turn your body* as you fall so you hit the ground with your side!

Incorrect B

Shawn releases Rodrigo's arm as he falls causing him to fall hard to the ground. Without the control of the arm, Rodrigo simply free falls. It is okay to do that once in a while, once you have mastered the break fall completely, but in training it is custom courtesy to control the fall so you don't have to land hard with every repetition. The proper way to do this is to execute the fall for a few repetitions with control. On the last repetition of the set, direct your partner to release you so you have to break a regular fall.

11

Standing forward roll

Another very important falling technique is the forward roll. There are instances in everyday life when you may have to use the forward roll and it may even save your life. One such experience Kid Peligro had was falling off a horse at full gallop. If he didn't know how to execute the forward roll he would have simply landed flat on the ground with severe consequences. As it was, he simply used the momentum and applied the forward roll and was able to roll forward a few times and absorb the fall without any ill consequences.

The best way to practice the forward roll is to begin slow and in control. Once you have mastered the move you can accelerate the rolling. Make sure you first practice technique #4, the shoulder roll, before you proceed with the standing forward roll.

1 Rodrigo begins the drill by standing with the right foot forward. His arms are down at the waist and his body is turned slightly to the left. Rodrigo takes a forward step with the right leg, toes pointing forward, and bends the knees slightly.

2 Rodrigo leans forward, bending at the waist, and bends the right leg. He pushes off the left leg as he plants the left hand on the ground. His left arm descends straight down from the shoulder and in line with his right foot. Rodrigo drives his right hand in between his legs and tucks his head in as if to touch the chest with the chin.

3 Rodrigo pushes off with the left leg, and rolls forward over his right shoulder. Notice that he uses the left hand on the ground to help control the move and ensure that he rolls over the right shoulder and not the head and spine. As he rolls forward, Rodrigo uses the break fall, landing on his left side; the open left arm hits the ground first to absorb the impact. Rodrigo tucks his left leg in and kicks the right leg over. He continues with the forward roll, using the forward momentum to propel him back up. While in the rolling motion, Rodrigo kneels on the left leg and plants the right foot forward and pushes off it to end in the same standing position as he started. Note that Rodrigo doesn't stop on the kneeling position. It is just a quick transitional stage as he rolls forward.

ADVANCED DRILLS

In this section Rodrigo presents a variety of advanced drills that both reinforce familiar techniques as well as introducing new ones. Be sure to pay close attention as some techniques are explained here inside some of the drills.

12

Side-to-side drill: Side-control

The side-control is a very stable and efficient position to launch attacks from and is made even more effective when you are able to switch sides and attack the opponent from the other direction.

This drill is a great drill to exercise your ability to switch sides and to transition to north-south position as well.

a

b

c

1 Rodrigo has perfect side control on Shawn from his right side. Rodrigo has his left arm wrapped under Shawn's head while his right arm wraps under Shawn's left arm and the hands are clasped together. Rodrigo changes the left arm from under Shawn's head and passes it in front until his hand grabs Shawn's left triceps. Rodrigo starts to move in a clockwise direction, planting the right hand on the mat next to Shawn's right hip to prevent him from moving his hips and escaping the control.

A

Details:

A Notice Rodrigo's right hand position: his hand is next to Shawn's right hip and prevents Shawn from moving to the right and following Rodrigo.

2 Rodrigo continues his clockwise motion. As he reaches north-south position he steps out with his left foot so his leg is straight, and presses his chest down on Shawn's chest to keep him flat on the mat. Rodrigo then kneels with his left knee next to Shawn's left side and brings his right leg around so his knee is next to Shawn's head. Rodrigo then wraps his right arm under Shawn's head and the left arm under Shawn's right arm and clasps his hands together reaching the mirror image of the start position. Rodrigo would then repeat the drill from side to side as many times as he feels necessary.

Details:

B Rodrigo uses his shoulder to press against Shawn's chin, forcing Shawn's head to turn away. By doing this Rodrigo prevents Shawn from turning into him to escape the position. Notice that his body follows the head, so by keeping the shoulder pushing Shawn's chin to the right Rodrigo prevents Shawn from turning to his left and facing him to escape the control.

13

Side-to-side drill: Knee on the stomach

Being able to change sides is always a good tool to have in Gracie Jiu-Jitsu. If you always attack from the same side your opponent will concentrate all his efforts on defending that side, but when you suddenly reverse and attack from the opposite side, you force him to divide his attention and also to completely change his defensive posture. In his transition to achieve his defensive posture on the opposite side, many times your opponent will yield openings for attacking. Rodrigo here demonstrates a knee on the stomach drill that not only develops your ability to transition from one side to the next but also works on the mount and the knee on the stomach position.

1 Rodrigo is on Shawn's right side in side-control position with his left hand grabbing Shawn's collar just behind the head and the right hand grabbing the belt on his right side. Pushing off his hands, Rodrigo springs up and slides his right knee over Shawn's stomach while stepping out with the left leg. Notice that Rodrigo's arms are extended and pulling up on Shawn's collar and belt while Rodrigo's knee presses down on the stomach, making it a very uncomfortable position for Shawn.

2 Rodrigo brings the left leg in with the knee touching Shawn's right hip. At the same time Rodrigo pivots on his right knee and loops his right leg over Shawn's knees until he lands mounted on Shawn. Notice Rodrigo's arms are open slightly wider than shoulder width with his hands planted on the ground to maintain the position. The key to the transition from side to side in this drill is to lean forward, putting your weight on the arms and making your hips and legs very light. This will help when jumping over the partner's legs.

a

3 Rodrigo pushes off his arms and springs up again, extending the right leg out and pivoting on the knee to loop the left leg over Shawn's knees, ending up with his knee on the stomach on the left side. Notice that although Rodrigo looped the left leg over Shawn's legs he kept the knee and shin on Shawn's stomach with the foot next to Shawn's right hip. Rodrigo then kneels next to Shawn and reaches side-control on the left side. Repeat the drill as many times as you feel necessary to get the motion down.

b

c

Detail:

Correct: To achieve maximum control and to make your opponent most uncomfortable in the knee on the stomach you need to pull up on his collar while you press down on the opposite hip to pin it to the ground while you drive your knee down into the stomach. Notice Rodrigo demonstrating the proper pressure with his right hand pulling Shawn's collar and the left hand pushing down on the right hip.

14

Side-to-side drill: Turtle

Another great side-to-side drill is from the turtle or all fours position. In this case, the opponent has turned turtle and Rodrigo circles over his back while maintaining pressure and looking for possible openings for attacks. Notice that Rodrigo changes the way he moves around Shawn: at times he switches the hips, other times he simply steps around with the legs out. Repeat the drill going from side to side and around in one direction then quickly reversing.

1 Rodrigo faces Shawn, who has turned turtle. Rodrigo's chest presses on Shawn's back to keep him pinned to the mat. Rodrigo pushes off his hands and pivots on his left foot as he steps his right leg back over the left, turning his hips so they are facing the same direction as Shawn. Rodrigo's left arm wraps around Shawn's back with the hand sliding in the space between Shawn's left leg and Rodrigo's arm grabbing his chest. Notice that Rodrigo maintains contact with his torso on Shawn's back at all times. He starts by rolling over his left side and pushes off the right foot to maintain constant pressure on the back. Rodrigo continues his clockwise movement by stepping with his left leg under the right until he ends up on Shawn's back.

2 Rodrigo changes his way of moving around Shawn as he continues to circle around Shawn. This time he keeps his hips pointing down instead of facing forward as he steps out with both legs, presses his chest against Shawn's back and takes steps around until he reaches the starting position again.

3 Rodrigo begins to circle back as he pivots off his right foot, loops the left leg over the right, then brings the right leg under the left again, ending on Shawn's back.

4 Rodrigo continues in the same direction (counter-clockwise) as he spreads his legs and walks around Shawn's left side until he reaches his head.

15

Fighting drill 1

This is one of the best and most complete fighting drills you can do in Gracie Jiu-Jitsu. In it you are going to replicate many of the most important elements of fighting from the top, including guard pass, mounting, and submissions. It is very important that you execute this drill slowly with a willing partner until you master the mechanics of the moves and the transitions between one move and the next. After mastering the moves and mechanics you can increase your speed. Remember speed is a consequence of repetition. Proper execution of the moves is much more important than speed. If you simply repeat the moves with no regard to proper mechanics then you are simply teaching your neuro-muscular system to execute the moves incorrectly. Rodrigo and Shawn help each other by allowing their movements to be completed to escape the submissions without undue pressure.

1 Rodrigo begins the drill inside Shawn's closed guard. Rodrigo has good posture – head and spine straight, the front arm gripping and controlling Shawn's collar at the chest, and his left arm controlling Shawn's hips. Rodrigo stands up by stepping forward first with his right leg and then the left and breaks Shawn's legs open. Notice Rodrigo's left elbow is inside Shawn's right thigh to avoid being triangled. Because this is a drill Rodrigo makes sure to use the proper mechanics at all times.

2 Rodrigo uses the stacking method to pass Shawn's guard. He wraps his right arm under and around Shawn's left leg until his hand grips Shawn's right collar. He then switches his left hand from Shawn's belt to behind his buttocks to prevent him from rolling and stacks his legs over his head and passes the guard.

3 Having reached side-control Rodrigo goes for the mount. With his left hand Rodrigo grabs Shawn's pants at the right hips so his left forearm is in front and blocking Shawn's hips. Rodrigo then slides his left knee over Shawn's hips and mounts him. Once he is mounted Rodrigo starts the submission part of the drill as slides his right hand inside Shawn's right collar, setting up the choke. At this point you can either apply the choke and start the drill over or continue the drill as follows.

4 Shawn uses his arms to block Rodrigo's choke with both hands, pulling down on Rodrigo's right forearm and setting up the possible upa escape. Rodrigo plants his left hand on the mat and shifts his hips to the left using his weight to counter the upa possibility to the right side (since his right arm is blocked by Shawn, that would be the side the upa would go to). Rodrigo changes to the double-attack and attacks Shawn's right arm.

5 Using his left arm as a brace and pivot point, Rodrigo slides his left knee up so it is right next to Shawn's right ear. His hips are at 90° with Shawn's body and trap the right arm. Rodrigo uses his right arm to control Shawn's right arm, and his left arm to pull up on Shawn's left arm to prevent him from turning to his left to escape the attack. Rodrigo plants his left hand in front of Shawn's left ear and pivots off that arm so he can lean to his right and bring his right leg towards Shawn's head, setting up the arm-lock. Rodrigo leans forward on the left arm with his body and loops his left leg around Shawn's head until his foot lands next to Shawn's left ear. Rodrigo then falls back for the arm-lock as he extends Shawn's right arm with his body so his hips push up against the elbow joint.

6 Having executed the arm-lock Rodrigo allows Shawn a little space so he can escape. Shawn practices his arm-lock escape as he turns his wrist counter-clockwise. Now his elbow is no longer pointing in the same direction as Rodrigo's hips, thus relieving the pressure. Shawn then pushes off his feet and bridges to his left shoulder while pushing Rodrigo's right leg open with the left hand. Shawn continues with the escape, pivoting his body around his right arm as he rolls over his left shoulder while using his feet to step to his left until he ends up on his knees next to Rodrigo's left side. Rodrigo transitions to the next submission. Rodrigo does not release his control over Shawn's right arm but allows him to twist the wrist and pivot around it. As Shawn reaches his left side Rodrigo bends his left leg and loops it over and around Shawn's right arm, setting up the omoplata.

7 Rodrigo continues with the omoplata as he wraps the left leg around Shawn's right arm and begins to sit forward to apply the pressure on Shawn's shoulder. Now it is Shawn's turn to escape: he grabs his own belt with the right hand, extends his right leg behind Rodrigo's back and pushes off it, bringing Rodrigo over him as he sits back down.

8 As Shawn completes his escape he ends up with Rodrigo in front of him and replaces the closed guard. They are now ready to repeat the drill.

Reverse View of 6, 7 & 8. Notice how Shawn rolls over his shoulders and uses his legs and hips to escape the arm-lock and the omoplata, and to replace the guard. As he rolls Rodrigo over to escape the omoplata he kicks his legs over his head and opens them up, framing Rodrigo inside them so he can keep him inside his guard and be able to close the legs.

16

Fighting drill 2

In this drill you and your partner will practice a sweep, mounting and guard replacement.

1 Rodrigo has Shawn in his closed guard with his right hand inside the right collar and the left hand controlling Shawn's right sleeves at the elbow. Rodrigo opens his legs and escape his hips to the right as he prepares for the scissors sweep. He drops the left leg to the ground next to Shawn's right leg while he bends his right leg and slides the knee in front of Shawn's hips until his shin is in front of Shawn's hips and his right foot hooks outside Shawn's left hip.

2 Rodrigo pulls up on Shawn's collar so his head leans forward, resting Shawn's weight on Rodrigo's right shin. Rodrigo then kicks his legs in a scissoring motion - his left leg kicks back while he kicks forward with his right, sweeping Shawn. Rodrigo follows Shawn as he falls and ends up mounted on him.

3 Shawn begins his guard replacement with the elbow escape. He turns to his left, slides his left elbow between his body and Rodrigo's right knee. He then loops his right leg over to the left with his foot landing just past Rodrigo's right ankle. In one motion Shawn pulls Rodrigo's right leg in with his own right leg as he coils and slides his left leg under Rodrigo's right knee. Shawn's left elbow and knee touch one another in the process to eliminate any space in which Rodrigo could regain the mount with his knee touching the ground. Having trapped Rodrigo's right leg in the half-guard (trapped with his right leg) Shawn turns his body to his right, escaping his hips to the left, and continues with the elbow escape. Shawn switches the leg trapping Rodrigo's right leg as he loops his left leg over, releasing the right leg to slide in front of Rodrigo's hips to complete the guard replacement. Shawn uses both hands on Rodrigo's left leg to brace and hold it in place, and coils the right leg while sliding his knee under Rodrigo's hips until it comes out in front of Rodrigo's left hip.

4 Shawn then moves his hips back to the right so he can create the space he needs to loop his right foot around Rodrigo's left leg and close the legs around his body to regain the closed guard. It is now Shawn's time to execute the drill. He starts by opening his legs, escaping the hips to the right and preparing the scissors sweep in the same manner that Rodrigo did and continues with the drill. You should practice this drill sweeping to both sides, either alternating with each repetition or working several times to one side and then repeating it to the other side for the same number of times.

Fighting drill 3: Submissions

This is a tremendous drill for submissions from the guard. Again make sure to execute the submission precisely but allow your partner to escape so you can flow into the next repetition.

1 Rodrigo begins the drill with Shawn in his closed guard. The first movement is an arm-lock from the guard: Rodrigo controls Shawn's right arm with his left arm, wrapping the forearm over the wrist and holding the lapel with his left hand to secure the grip. Rodrigo opens his guard and slips his right arm inside Shawn's legs, hooking behind the left leg as he uses the arm to help pull his torso to the right while his legs move his hips to the left.

2 Rodrigo continues to pull his torso to the right with his right arm until his body is at 90° with Shawn's. At the same time he brings his right leg over Shawn's back behind the left armpit and swings his left leg up and around Shawn's head to lock in the arm-lock. Rodrigo extends his body while lifting his hips to apply the arm-lock pressure just slightly so he can feel the submission.

3 The next movement is a triangle: Rodrigo quickly releases the pressure on Shawn's right arm, allowing him to yank his arm out and escape the hold. Rodrigo grabs Shawn's left sleeve at the wrist with his left hand, places his right foot on Shawn's left hip and pushes off it to re-center his body. Rodrigo swings the left leg up and over Shawn's right shoulder.

4 Rodrigo locks the left leg over Shawn's right shoulder, bending it at the knee while at the same time he pulls Shawn's left arm across his body with his left hand. Notice Rodrigo's left calf pressing down on the back of Shawn's head, preventing him from raising his torso to counter the attack. Rodrigo grabs his own left shin with the right hand and loops the right leg over it, locking the figure 4 around Shawn's left arm and head for the triangle and presses his knees together to feel the submission.

5 The next movement is the omoplata or shoulder lock: Rodrigo releases his left hand grip on Shawn's left sleeve, allowing him to escape the triangle. Shawn moves his left arm to his own left and across Rodrigo's body to defend the submission. Rodrigo reaches with his left hand and grabs Shawn's gi at the left shoulder.

6 Rodrigo releases the triangle lock and swings his torso to the right while looping his right leg around Shawn's left arm. Rodrigo uses his right hand to grab Shawn's belt to assist pulling his torso parallel to Shawn's and to prevent Shawn from rolling forward to escape the submission. Rodrigo drives both legs down to the mat forcing Shawn to fall forward flat on the mat.

7 Rodrigo releases his right hand grip on Shawn's belt and wraps that arm around Shawn's waist as he sits further forward. Rodrigo bends both legs back as he continues to apply torque on Shawn's left shoulder. Again Rodrigo makes sure he feels the submission before allowing Shawn to counter it.

8 Shawn counters the omoplata by grabbing his own belt with his left hand. At this point Rodrigo's right leg is still wrapped around Shawn's left arm. He then opens his left leg wide behind Rodrigo's back and rolls towards his right side, pulling Rodrigo over the top of him and using his right hand on Rodrigo's left leg to help him over the top.

9 Rodrigo lands on all fours next to Shawn's left side. Shawn continues the drill by swinging his body to his right while looping his right leg over Rodrigo's head so he has Rodrigo between his legs. Shawn then closes the legs around Rodrigo's hips to end up in closed guard. Now Shawn is ready to do the drill on Rodrigo.

Fighting drill 4: Guard replacement, one hand tied

In the next two drills Rodrigo plays open guard with first one, then both hands grabbing his own belt to learn to use his feet as hooks to prevent Shawn from passing the guard. After you have repeated these drills a few times you can ad lib. It is not so important to follow the steps as presented but more to get the general idea of the drill and flow freely between each movement as you create your own drill. Once you have mastered the use of the hooks and you can use both hands to stop your opponent, your guard is going to be much more effective.

1 Rodrigo begins with Shawn in his open guard. Rodrigo grabs his belt with the left hand to add difficulty to the drill. His right hand grabs Shawn's right sleeve, and his left foot presses on Shawn's right hip while his right leg pushes on Shawn's left biceps. As Shawn circles to his left, he grips and controls both of Rodrigo's legs by holding the gi pants. Rodrigo moves his right leg from pushing against the biceps to grapevining around the outside of Shawn's left leg. Rodrigo changes his right hand from Shawn's left sleeve and grabs behind the left ankle instead.

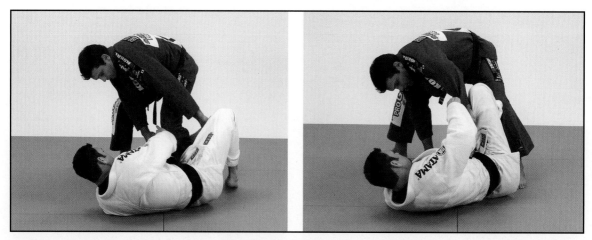

2 Shawn counters Rodrigo's defense by pushing down on Rodrigo's left leg with his right hand while taking a step to his own right. Rodrigo swings his torso to the left and places his right hand on Shawn's left knee to block his pass temporarily. This allows Rodrigo enough time to loop the right leg around Shawn's left leg so his right foot hooks in front of the knee, stopping Shawn's forward progress. Rodrigo pushes off his right foot hook to swing his body back to center and away from Shawn.

Fighting drill 5: Guard replacement, both hands tied

In this case, to further develop the use of his legs and feet in the open guard, Rodrigo grabs his belt with both hands.

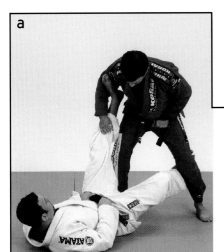

1 Shawn grips Rodrigo's left gi pants near the ankle and straightens his body to relieve Rodrigo's foot pressure on the biceps. Once he releases the pressure Shawn pushes Rodrigo's foot down and to his left to pin Rodrigo's legs down. Rodrigo quickly reacts and circles his left leg around Shawn's right leg until he hooks his left foot just behind Shawn's knee.

2 Shawn pushes Rodrigo's left leg down to release the hook and drives it over to his left in his *attempt* to pass. Rodrigo rolls over his right shoulder until he is on all fours to stop the pass.

3 Rodrigo pushes off his right foot and swings the left leg out and over his body as he rolls back over his shoulder until he faces Shawn. Rodrigo loops his left leg over Shawn's right arm until he hooks the foot inside Shawn's right arm. At the same time he places his right foot on Shawn's left biceps, completing the drill. Rodrigo continues with the drill towards his left side.

TECHNIQUES AND TECHNICAL INSIGHTS

The following pages present techniques and deeper insights and the mechanics of leverage and details that apply in many techniques in Jiu-Jitsu. By fully understanding the mechanics of these principles you will be able to adjust and correct a large number of techniques that you have already learned. You will also be able to figure out how to solve future techniques as you face them for the first time, and ascertain what is important for them to work.

Mount escape: Upa or bridge

The mounted position is perhaps one of the worst positions one can find himself in. Being able to quickly and effectively escape from it is a skill every Jiu-Jitsu student must learn. The upa or bridge escape is a basic maneuver that must be mastered for anyone with plans of advancing beyond the rank of white belt. Rodrigo recommends that you use this move as a drill prior to every training session. This two-person drill uses a similar movement pattern to the second drill in this book, turning to your knees.

1 To best understand the situation and the escape it is important to realize what Shawn needs to maintain his position. In the mount, Shawn needs his arms to keep him on top. If Rodrigo pushes Shawn to the right Shawn braces with the right arm and stops the motion. If Rodrigo pushes him to the left Shawn braces with the left arm. If Shawn holds his arms back Rodrigo can pull him and drive him to any side he wants and reverse the position. So the key to escaping and reversing is to always realize what the opponent needs to maintain the position and then destroy those elements. In the case of the mount, Rodrigo needs to block all the bracing options that Shawn has to one side and then reverse him to that side.

2 Shawn is mounted on Rodrigo with his right hand in the collar, setting up a possible choke. Rodrigo hooks Shawn's right wrist with his right hand in a claw (all fingers together on the same side). He pulls the wrist towards his right to create some space between Shawn's wrist and his neck, taking away some of the effectiveness of a possible choke that Shawn could attempt. Rodrigo makes sure to have his elbow tight against his ribs for maximum power. With his left hand Rodrigo grabs Shawn's right gi sleeve at the shoulder, controlling Shawn's right arm and preventing him from pulling it out to brace. Notice Rodrigo's left elbow is tight against his side as well, giving him more power. At the same time Rodrigo loops his left foot over Shawn's right foot, trapping the right leg and preventing Shawn from opening it out to brace.

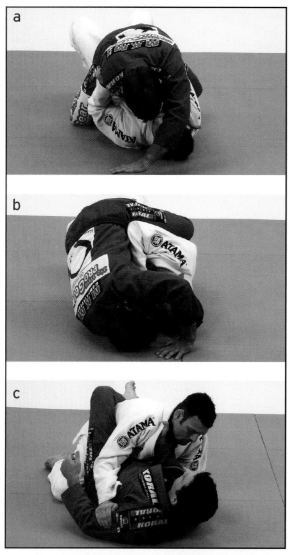

Side view of the whole move
Notice Rodrigo trapping Shawn's right foot by looping his own left foot over it. Also notice Rodrigo's leg scissoring motion creating the added momentum for the reversal.

3 Having effectively trapped Shawn's right side to keep him from being able to brace, Rodrigo will execute the bridge and roll to that side. Rodrigo pushes off both feet, bridging straight up and driving Shawn's head towards the mat. At the highest point of the bridge Rodrigo pushes off his left foot and kicks the right leg over towards the left, rolling his body over to the left and reversing the position. Once Rodrigo completely reverses the position he ends up inside Shawn's closed guard. Rodrigo makes sure to place his right hand on Shawn's left biceps to block him from using that hand to choke him. It is very common for beginners to forget to block the biceps after they execute the escape, ending up choked from the closed guard. To continue the drill Shawn would release the closed guard and allow Rodrigo to step over the legs and mount him.

3 Incorrect: Notice that since Rodrigo trapped Shawn's right side he needs to bridge and roll to that side, if he tries to go to the opposite side, in this case Shawn's left, Shawn can simply open his arm, brace and stop the roll.

Side control escape

Being on the bottom with the opponent in side-control is another very common position one finds himself in during sparring sessions or competition. The side control position offers a lot of stability for the person on top and being able to escape and replace the block between you and your opponent is extremely important as well. Notice that Rodrigo uses the hip escape motion (drill #1) to escape the side-control.

1 Shawn has side control on Rodrigo. His right arm is wrapped under Rodrigo's head and the left is wrapped under Rodrigo's right arm.

2 Rodrigo pushes off his right foot and escapes his hips to his right until he has enough space to be able to coil his left leg and bring the knee in front of Shawn's hips.

2 **Reverse and Detail:** Notice Rodrigo's arm and hand position. His arms are bent at approximately 90°. The left forearm is braced against Shawn's hips, preventing Shawn from getting his hips too close to Rodrigo which would make the escape and being able to slide the left knee in more difficult. Rodrigo's right hand is pressed against Shawn's right chest with the forearm bent (it can also be pushing against Shawn's throat), which also keeps Shawn at a distance. Note that Rodrigo's bent arms are extremely important for two reasons: first, the left elbow blocks Shawn's hips and second, the right elbow blocks Shawn's left shoulder – both preventing Shawn from closing the distance.

2 **Detail:** Notice Rodrigo's proper posture and movement in isolation. The arms are bent with the elbows at 90°. The right foot on the ground gives him the ability to escape his hips to the right. Also notice how Rodrigo's left leg is cocked at an angle with the foot higher than the knee. This is another very important detail: by bringing the left foot up, Rodrigo is able to point the knee down and in so as to slip it in front of the opponent's hips. The diagonal angle of the leg also requires less space to be able to clear the opponent's body in case he has his knees forward. This allows Rodrigo's left knee to slide right in front of the opponent's hipbone.

2 **Incorrect:** Rodrigo incorrectly extends his arms fully to keep Shawn away. Without the elbows to prevent him from turning his body, Shawn simply twists the hips, stepping forward with the left leg, and regains side control.

22

Side control escape alternative: Bridge-hip escape combination

An even more effective way to escape side-control involves combining the hip escape with the bridge technique. This option is one of the most effective of the side control escapes and should be the best choice when the opponent is applying pressure with his chest against your chest. When using the two escapes in combination, you will create a lot more space, as the bridge will move the opponent away allowing for an easier hip escape and knee insertion. The same concept of upa-hip escape is used in escaping the mounted position.

1 Shawn has side control on Rodrigo. Rodrigo pushes off both feet and bridges, thrusting his hips up. The force of Rodrigo's hips going up pushes Shawn up towards Rodrigo's head.

a

b

c

2 At the height of the bridging movement, Rodrigo prepares the hip escape. He extends his right leg out and turns his body to the right. As Rodrigo begins to drop his hips down, he combines the turning movement with the hip escape and pushes off his left foot while moving his hips to the left. Rodrigo coils the right leg and drives the knee in front of Shawn's hips. At this point Rodrigo's right elbow and knee touch one another to form a block starting with Rodrigo's right forearm to the elbow continuing with the knee and the shin, making it impossible for Shawn to get close to Rodrigo's right side. Rodrigo then re-centers his body and traps Shawn's right leg by looping the left foot over it, effectively replacing the guard.

The bridge and hip escape without the opponent.

Notice Rodrigo's arms position – arms curled at the elbows. Also notice how Rodrigo prepares the hip escape at the height of the bridge by extending the right leg and turning his body to the right.

23

Frame

A very important technical position that is not commonly explained is the frame. The frame is used in various escape situations in Gracie Jiu-Jitsu, such as mount escape, head-lock escape, side control escape, among others. The importance of correctly understanding the mechanics of the frame cannot be overstated because of the role that a correctly applied frame plays in so many situations.

1 Rodrigo's body is turned to his right side, his right leg is flat on the mat and the left leg is bent with the foot firmly planted on the mat. His right arm is bent at the elbow with the elbow firmly braced against the mat. Rodrigo's left arm is also bent at the elbow at 90° to complete the frame. Since Rodrigo is turned to his right his right hand grips the left wrist with the forearm perpendicular to the ground. The arm position ensures that any weight applied on the top of the frame (Rodrigo's left forearm) is transferred directly down to the mat through Rodrigo's right forearm. Notice that Rodrigo does not have to exert any force to maintain the frame. Also notice that should he have used the left hand to grip the right wrist, all the weight applied to the left forearm would force the left hand to slide down the right arm.

1 **Incorrect frame:** Rodrigo extends his arms, raising the right elbow and arm off the mat. By doing this Rodrigo removes the ability to directly transfer the load to the mat and has to support it with his arms instead.

2 **The frame applied correctly:** Rodrigo's left forearm receives Shawn's weight and transfers it down to the mat through the right arm.

2 **The frame applied incorrectly:** Because Rodrigo's arms are extended, Shawn can easily deflect the frame by driving his body up. Also, Rodrigo has to support Shawn's weight with his arms instead of simply allowing the frame to transfer the weight to the ground.

Demonstration of the importance of the proper frame:

Notice that on figure A Rodrigo's forearm supports Shawn's weight without any effort on Rodrigo's part. Rodrigo can maintain this position forever. On figure B Rodrigo has to support Shawn's weight with his arms using his own power. Rodrigo would eventually tire and have to give up the brace. By using the proper framing technique one can find power and comfort in various situations. Look for similar applications in other Jiu-Jitsu positions.

Side control escape: Turning to your knees

Another option to escape side control is using the same movement as techniques #2 and #3, turning to your knees or all fours. This generally works best when the opponent is not applying a lot of pressure with his chest on your chest, such as when the side control is not fully established or when the opponent is transitioning to an attack or switching position to the other side.

1 Shawn has side control on Rodrigo but has not established full chest to chest pressure. Rodrigo plants his right foot on the ground and turns his body to the left while sliding his right arm under Shawn left arm and coiling the left arm in.

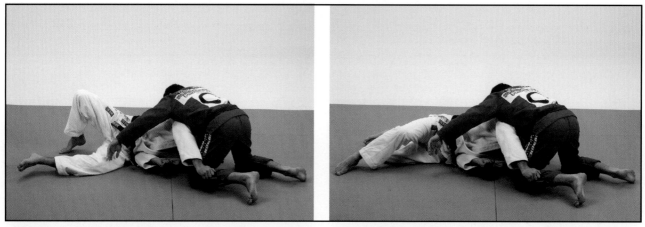

2 Rodrigo steps out with the right foot to help his hips move to the left. He then quickly scissors the legs, bringing the left leg under the right. He uses the momentum of the movement to help turn his body towards the left. At this time Rodrigo also grips Shawn's left pant leg with the right arm, preventing Shawn from moving around Rodrigo's head and reaching his back.

3 Rodrigo continues turning to his left until he ends up on his knees facing Shawn.

Forearm use to control distance

A very important consideration in Gracie Jiu-Jitsu is the concept of distance. In order for your opponent to attempt a submission, reach a controlling position or execute a strike against you he has to be able to get close. Using the forearm to control distance is a very effective way to avoid such situations. Rodrigo here demonstrates a few instances where he uses his forearms to control the opponent and maintain distance by intercepting the biceps or torso. Note that although he is just showing a few examples, the same principle occurs in many other positions, so be on the lookout for them and apply the principle wherever you see the opportunity.

A From side control: Rodrigo's right hand cups around Shawn's left triceps preventing Shawn from reaching with his left arm around Rodrigo's head to control it. Notice Rodrigo's hand and arm position: the hand actually grips Shawn's triceps just above the elbow with the forearm blocking the biceps and the arm from advancing near Rodrigo's head. Should Shawn be able to wrap the arm around Rodrigo's head he would have a lot of control over Rodrigo's torso. By keeping Shawn's arm from wrapping, Rodrigo is able to move his own hips and torso to escape or replace the guard.

B From side control Incorrect: Rodrigo places the right hand in front of Shawn's left biceps. Since Rodrigo doesn't use the forearm as a wide block Shawn is able to loop his arm over Rodrigo's head and reach head control.

C From the closed guard: Rodrigo places his hand on Shawn's triceps using his weight to trap the arms. In this case because the ground prevents Shawn from moving the arm back, Rodrigo cups the hand grabbing Shawn's triceps and drives his elbow down towards the mat, again using the forearm in front of the biceps to prevent Shawn from attacking. Since he cannot use his hands to grab a collar or use both arms to secure one arm, Shawn is incapable of applying chokes, arm-locks or even trying to punch Rodrigo's face.

D **From the closed guard Incorrect:** Rodrigo's elbows are not pointing down towards the mat. Without the forearm block Shawn is able to circle his arms under Rodrigo's arm and can grip Rodrigo's collar or arm for an arm-lock.

E **From the closed guard:** In this case since Rodrigo has posture with his back straight and his head away from Shawn's torso, Rodrigo can simply place his right hand on Shawn's left biceps to block that hand from reaching the collar and completing the grip for a possible choke. Rodrigo can allow one hand to grab his collar (in this case Shawn's right hand), what he cannot is allow both hands to grab the collar, which sets up the choke.

F **Side control:** Notice Rodrigo's right and left forearm blocking Shawn from getting close. Rodrigo's left hand placed on Shawn's left shoulder with the arm bent at 90° places his left forearm at the perfect angle to block Shawn's head and torso from closing the distance. At the same time Rodrigo's right forearm with the right hand at Shawn's left rib keeps distance on the lower part of the torso.

G Rodrigo uses the forearm to block Shawn's punch.

H Rodrigo grabs Shawn's left triceps with his right hand and drops the elbow down, using the forearm to block Shawn's ability to gain a good grip in the standing fight.

Leg use to control distance

Another way to control the distance between you and your opponent, especially when fighting from the bottom, is to use your legs to maintain the distance. Here Rodrigo demonstrates various situations in which he uses his legs to maintain the proper distance between himself and his opponent. Notice that the proper distance varies with his intent. There is a distance if he wants to sweep and there is a different distance if he wants to avoid being kicked and yet even another one if he simply wants to prevent his opponent from passing his guard. Look at the general principles of Rodrigo's usage of his legs and apply the principles to other situations.

A Rodrigo uses his extended left leg, foot pressed against Shawn's hips, to prevent Shawn from getting near and passing his guard. With the leg extended Rodrigo hardly needs to use any effort to keep Shawn at a distance.

B Should Shawn stand up and attempt to pass standing, the same leg position will continue to maintain the distance.

C If Shawn insists on pressing forward Rodrigo can quickly curl his legs allowing Shawn to fall forward. Rodrigo quickly extends his legs again, lifting Shawn off the mat for a sweep.

D Rodrigo places his left foot on Shawn's right hip to prevent him from getting close in his guard passing attempt. When Rodrigo extends the leg he creates even more distance between himself and Shawn.

E Rodrigo uses his left knee to block Shawn's right leg from coming forward. Again Rodrigo doesn't have to use any strength to keep Shawn at a distance. When he is able to put the knee in front, all Shawn's power is transferred to Rodrigo's femur, creating an effective block.

F Rodrigo slides his right knee in front of Shawn's stomach so his shin blocks Shawn's hips from coming forward.

DEALING WITH THE STIFF ARM

The stiff arm occurs everywhere in Jiu-Jitsu. It can be a formidable weapon to maintain space temporarily and can create a difficult barrier to overcome if you don't know how to deal with it. Rodrigo stated that if you are using power you are not using Gracie Jiu-Jitsu, so when you are faced with a stiff arm, don't simply try to muscle your way past it. Your opponent is using a more efficient platform than you, so he doesn't have to exert much power to maintain the

stiff arm barrier. You, on the other hand, are using a great deal of energy to try to push through it. The obvious solution, and it should be a solution you should seek in many other situations, is to simply deflect the power by using your body. Rodrigo here demonstrates a series of stiff arms situations and how to deflect them. Many other "barriers" can be dealt with in the same manner in Gracie Jiu-Jitsu.

Passing the guard

1 Rodrigo attempts to pass Shawn's guard and reach side control but Shawn
stops him with the stiff arms pushing against Rodrigo's chest.

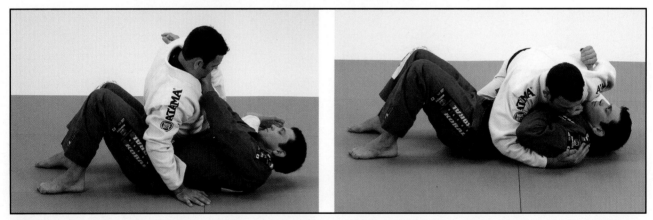

2 Rather than fight against the stiff arm, Rodrigo simply switches the hips and deflects the power. Rodrigo shoots the right leg
forward and under the left one turning his hips counter-clockwise so he can deflect Shawn's stiff arm and get closer to the head.
Once he breaks the barrier Rodrigo switches the hips back again and secures side control.

Mounted position 1: Arms push up

1 Rodrigo is mounted on Shawn but Shawn counters by pushing with both arms against Rodrigo's chest. Although a good option here may be to simply execute an arm-lock on one of the arms, many times you may prefer to maintain the mount. For example, in a street fight you may not want to take a chance and go for the arm-lock only to have it fail and end up on the bottom.

2 Rodrigo turns his shoulders to the left and slides the right hand inside Shawn's left arm, aiming the hand towards the left side of Shawn's head. As Rodrigo turns his shoulders back to the right, his right arm deflects Shawn's left arm of his chest. At the same time, Rodrigo slides his left arm inside Shawn's right arm and repeats the motion in the opposite direction (i.e. rotates the shoulders to the left) to deflect that arm.

Mounted position 2: Arms push the knees

1 Rodrigo is mounted on Shawn but Shawn manages to get his left arm on Rodrigo's right knee and pushes off it. If Rodrigo doesn't react Shawn will escape the mount or at least keep Rodrigo's body down and away from the best mount (knees are up and under Shawn's armpits).

2 Rodrigo reaches with his right hand in a claw grip, with all five fingers together, and cups under Shawn's left wrist and pulls it up deflecting Shawn's power away from his knee.

CHOKES

Grandmaster Helio Gracie likes to say that "There may be strong arms but there are no strong necks!" By cutting the blood flow to the brain, the choke simply "turns out the lights" on the opponent regardless of how strong or determined he or she may be, making them the premiere choice of submission for a Gracie Jiu-Jitsu fighter. One of the most important keys to a successful choke, besides the technical part of course, is the amount of pressure you use to choke. Many times beginners will use all of their strength in applying the choke, only to have their hands tire and slowly release the grip before the opponent submits. This occurs especially against tough opponents who have good neck strength and good defense. The key is to execute a constant pressure that you can sustain. It is better to go 80%, then 85% of your maximum and let the choke do its job of depleting the blood flow to the brain, rather than try to use 110% of your power hoping for the quick submission only to "burn" your grip and then have to release it before your opponent submits or passes out.

Basic collar choke: Standard grip

The collar choke from the guard is one of the most effective chokes in Gracie Jiu-Jitsu. It needs to be mastered so that when properly executed it will either yield a submission or draw enough of your opponent's resources and attention to defend it, opening other opportunities such as sweeps and other submissions. The standard grip involves sliding the second hand under the first hand. Although it is a little more difficult to use at the highest levels it is still an important choke variation to master.

1 Rodrigo has Shawn in his closed guard. He opens Shawn's right lapel with his left hand pulling it down slightly to tighten it so he can slide the right hand up the collar with his four fingers inside, keeping the thumb on the outside of the collar.

2 Rodrigo opens his legs and using the pressure of his thighs against Shawn's hips he turns his torso to the left. Rodrigo slides his left hand under the right arm, gripping the inside of Shawn's left collar. Notice that by turning his torso to the left Rodrigo raises his right elbow allowing a better angle and more space for his left hand to slide under. Once Rodrigo secures the proper choking grip he re-centers his body, closes the guard and applies the choking pressure by pulling Shawn's head down to his chest with his hands while driving the elbows to the mat for greater pressure.

Choke details:

A Rodrigo curls his hands as if he is wringing a towel. This curling motion tightens Shawn's collar around his neck. When properly done this motion alone may be enough to choke most people. The direction of the curl is inward, as if he wanted to see the knuckles of his hands.

B Correct: When Rodrigo curls the hands properly he places the narrow blade of his forearm against Shawn's neck. The narrower blade creates a greater amount of pressure, much like when you use the edge of a knife rather than the flat side to cut an object.

B Incorrect: Rodrigo doesn't curl the wrists and has the wide part of his forearm pressing against Shawn's neck, making the choke a lot weaker.

30

Basic collar choke: Top grip

In this version of the basic collar choke Rodrigo uses a faster variation called the top grip. This is version is a quicker attack since you don't need to slide the second hand under the first one, making it a bit easier to reach the choking position than the standard grip.

1 Rodrigo has Shawn in his closed guard. Rodrigo uses his right hand to grip Shawn's right collar with the four fingers on the inside and the thumb on the outside. In order to have the tightest choke Rodrigo tries to have his hand as far behind Shawn's head as possible.

1 **Detail:** Rodrigo uses the left hand to open the lapel allowing the right hand to slide further up towards the back of Shawn's neck. Also notice Rodrigo's grip: the four fingers inside and the thumb out. Rodrigo's arm is bent with the elbow pointing in towards the center of his stomach.

2 Rodrigo opens his legs and using the pressure of the thighs against Shawn's hips as a fulcrum moves his torso to the right so he can easily reach Shawn's left shoulder with his left hand. Rodrigo tries to grip the gi at the shoulder with his left hand as close to his right one as possible. Rodrigo re-centers his body and closes the guard again. Rodrigo tightens the choke by pulling the Shawn's collar towards his chest and driving his elbows to the mat.

2 Detail: Notice how Rodrigo grabs the outside top of Shawn's gi near the left shoulder. This allows for a quicker choke than trying to slip the left hand inside the left collar.

2 Incorrect: Rodrigo tries to tighten the choke with his arms extended as he opens up his elbows. This not only has less pressure than pulling the elbows down but it is also very easy to defend by using the hands to push the elbows down.

Side view of the choking motion.
Notice how Rodrigo pulls Shawn's collar towards his chest. Rodrigo uses his legs to help bring Shawn's torso forward, forcing the chest close to Rodrigo's chest.

31

Mata-leao, or rear naked choke

The mata-leao, or the rear naked choke, is perhaps the most versatile and devastating submission in all of Gracie Jiu-Jitsu. The mata-leao is not a collar choke so it works equally well in a submission wrestling match, a street fight or a MMA match. Like every technique in the art, proper mechanics make a difference between success and failure, so pay close attention to the details.

1 Rodrigo has Shawn's back with his hooks applied to Shawn's hips. Rodrigo wraps his right arm around Shawn's neck with the right hand grasping Shawn's left shoulder.

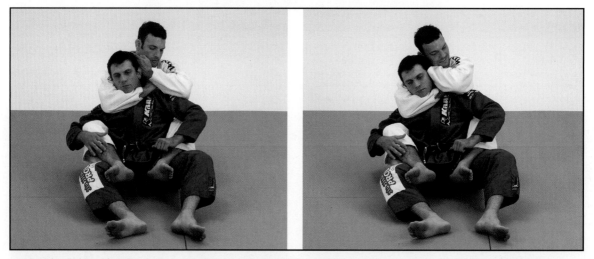

2 Rodrigo brings his left hand up and slides it between Shawn's head and his own head, the palm toward his face. Rodrigo then slides his right hand inside his own left arm so that the hand grabs the left biceps. Rodrigo applies the choking pressure by bringing his elbows together as he drives his head forward squeezing Shawn's neck.

Choke details:

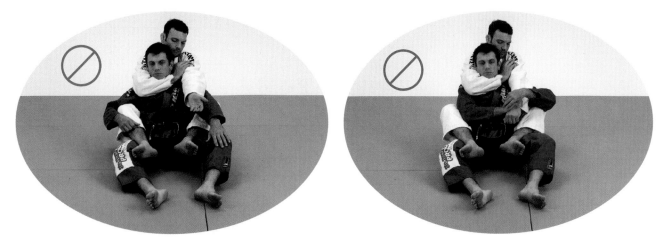

A **Incorrect:** This is a very common execution mistake: as Rodrigo wraps the right arm around Shawn's neck, he extends the left arm so he can lock the right hand over the left biceps *before* sliding the left hand on the back of Shawn's neck. As you can see, Shawn can easily block the choke by grabbing Rodrigo's extended left arm with his hands. In some cases, if Rodrigo's elbow is pointing down, Shawn can even execute an arm-bar on Rodrigo's left arm by pulling the forearm down, forcing the elbow against his left shoulder.

B **Incorrect:** Instead of sliding his left hand between their heads, Rodrigo drapes his left hand on top of Shawn's head. In this case Shawn can easily defend the choke by reaching with his hands, grabbing Rodrigo's fingers and prying Rodrigo's hand from his head, releasing the choke.

32

Cross collar choke

The cross collar is another effective choke when you control your opponent's back. By using the gi collars and proper arm position, you can generate a lot of pressure for a devastating choke. In most cases of chokes from the back-mount, in order for you to develop sufficient leverage, you have to have one arm under the opponent's arm and the other over his opposite arm.

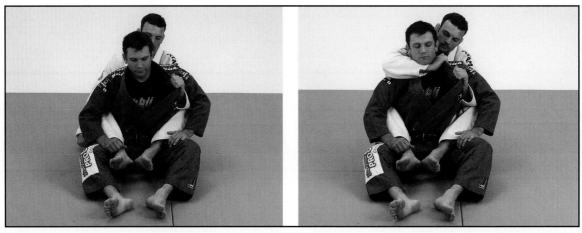

1 Rodrigo has Shawn's back with his feet hooked on Shawn's hips for control. Rodrigo slides his left arm under Shawn's left arm and grabs and opens Shawn's left collar as he reaches with the right arm around Shawn's neck and grabs the top of the collar. Notice how Rodrigo pulls Shawn's left collar down and out to tighten it and make it easy for his right hand to grip as high up the collar as possible.

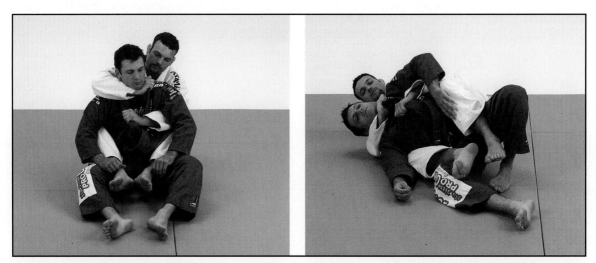

2 Once he has a firm grip on Shawn's left collar Rodrigo changes his left hand from the left collar and grabs the right collar instead. This second collar grip does not have to be as tight as the first one as it is going to be used to tighten the choke. Once he has his hands set, Rodrigo falls to the right and chokes Shawn by pulling down on Shawn's right lapel with his left hand and pulling up Shawn's left lapel with the right hand. Rodrigo's arm motion is as if he were pulling a bow (left hand) and arrow (right hand) to shoot.

Choke details:

A **Correct:** Notice how Rodrigo twists Shawn's collar as he opens it. This way his hand grips the collar in a double mode instead of just a straight grip, making it a lot harder to break the grip and also making the collar turn into a blade. Check out Rodrigo's hand grip: his fingers actually wrap around the collar, turning the top to the left as his thumb reaches inside to complete the grip.

B **Incorrect:** Notice that this time Rodrigo did not turn Shawn's collar. His grip is straight across, making it easier to slip out and, most important, not as effective a choke.

C Rodrigo grabs Shawn's right lapel with the left hand. The arm goes under Shawn's arm so he can generate leverage for the choke as he pulls down with that arm.

D Rodrigo demonstrates the proper angle of his right hand. The correct angle makes the hand act like a knife cutting Shawn's throat.

33

Triangle

Another important and basic submission is the triangle choke. Many times fighters complain or argue that the triangle choke doesn't work quite well, especially if you have short legs. Others argue that the choke is easy to defend with good posture and a myriad of other escapes. Rodrigo disagrees – if you train yourself in the proper details and nuances to execute the perfect triangle you will find it will work for anyone and against anyone.

1 Rodrigo places his right foot on Shawn's hips while controlling his left arm and loops his left leg over Shawn's right arm.

2 Rodrigo pushes off his right foot, moving his body back away from Shawn forcing him to fall forward. Rodrigo starts to turn his body to the left as he uses his left hand to pull Shawn's left arm across his body. At the same time, he adjusts his left leg so that his calf presses down on the back of Shawn's neck, preventing him from raising his torso and regaining posture. One of the major mistakes people make when executing the triangle is to fail to control the opponent's posture. Rodrigo's foot against the hips allows him to break Shawn's posture and force his torso to lean forward. This makes it easy to pull the left arm across and adjust his left leg over the back of Shawn's neck. Had Rodrigo not pushed away and forced Shawn to lean forward as much as he has it would be difficult, even impossible, for him to make these adjustments.

3 Rodrigo reaches with his right hand and holds his own left shin, further securing the triangle trap around Shawn's left arm and head. Notice that Rodrigo maintains pressure with his right foot against Shawn's hips to maintain the distance and prevent Shawn from raising his head and torso to regain posture and defend the triangle.

4 Rodrigo locks his right leg over the left calf for the figure 4 triangle on Shawn. Rodrigo points to his leg to show the proper way to lock the triangle: the toes of his left foot are up, making sure he locks his right leg *over the left shin and not the left foot* otherwise he risks breaking the foot should the opponent somehow quickly rise up.

4 **Front view:** Notice how Rodrigo pulls Shawn's left arm across his body. This sets up the proper angle for the choke and also allows him an easier path to loop his left leg over Shawn's head.

5 To finalize the move and add pressure to the choke, Rodrigo uses both hands to pull down on Shawn's head while he squeezes his knees together.

5 **Front view:** Rodrigo points in the direction of the pressure exerted by his knees on the choke. Notice how Shawn's left arm, pulled across presses into the left side of his throat.

Incorrect: Common mistakes when executing the triangle

A Rodrigo puts his right foot on the ground and tries to loop his left leg over Shawn's right arm. Shawn is not forced out of his posture, making it very hard for Rodrigo to loop his leg over the back of Shawn's neck. Only someone with very long legs could complete the maneuver.

B Since Rodrigo wasn't able to lock his left leg on the back of Shawn's neck, he cannot push down with it to keep Shawn from raising his head. When Rodrigo tries to lock his feet together for the triangle Shawn simply raises his torso, gaining posture and foiling Rodrigo's ability to properly lock his legs in the figure 4. Shawn is in perfect position to pass Rodrigo's guard: he simply reaches over and passes Rodrigo's guard using the stacking method.

C Rodrigo locks his right leg over his extended left foot. When Shawn fights to escape he raises his torso, putting such pressure on Rodrigo's left foot that it may break.

Triangle details:

The following instructions illustrate importance of applying proper pressure in the right location to prevent the opponent from gaining posture.

Incorrect:
If his leg is not pressing down on the back of Shawn's head Shawn can easily raise his torso. To illustrate the point Rodrigo places his hand on the middle of Shawn's back. Without pressure on the back of his head Shawn easily raises his torso.

Incorrect:
Even when the pressure is a little higher up Shawn may still be able to raise his torso.

Correct: With the pressure in the correct spot (back of the neck) Rodrigo points out that Shawn cannot raise his torso.

34

Triangle: Opponent gains posture

If Rodrigo finds he cannot move his hips away and Shawn is able to partially raise his torso, Rodrigo will break Shawn's his posture by pulling the back of the head as demonstrated in the previous technique.

1 Rodrigo closes his feet around Shawn's back but Shawn is able to raise his torso and gain a little posture.

2 Rodrigo uses his left hand to pull down on Shawn's head, breaking his posture.

3 While still holding the back of Shawn's head and pulling the left arm across to prevent Shawn from pulling out, Rodrigo unlocks his feet and places his right foot on Shawn's left hip.

Rodrigo grabs his left shin with his right hand to maintain the lock around Shawn's arm and head and loops his right foot over the left shin to lock the figure 4 triangle. Rodrigo applies pressure by pulling Shawn's head down with both hands while he closes his knees together.

JOINT SUBMISSION TIPS

Proper mechanics are very important in every aspect of Gracie Jiu-Jitsu. In submission attempts, the proper mechanics such as hip position, grips, tightness, angles of the leg and body in relation to the opponent greatly affect the outcome and success of any submission attempt. In general, when a submission is directed towards a joint, the attacker's hip needs to be as close to that joint as possible for best results.

Tightness against the limb that you are attacking is of paramount concern so Rodrigo will give you general tips for best success in joint submissions. In these cases Rodrigo demonstrates a foot-lock, an arm-lock from the side, the shoulder-locks (omoplata) and the key-lock (Americana) but the same principles apply to arm-locks from other positions like knee bars.

Foot-lock

The foot-lock is a great submission attack and when properly applied can end a fight quickly. But even in the event that the opponent escapes, just the mere threat of his feet being attacked will affect his game for the rest of the match. The foot-lock can be applied from various positions so it is a very versatile submission. There are some things to keep in mind however when attempting a foot-lock. First, some people have much greater range of motion on their feet than others and it may be very hard to submit them with a foot-lock. Second, in general, you should not attempt a foot-lock on opponents who are much taller than you – the length of their leg being much longer than yours will affect your ability to apply the pressure on the joint. Third, when going for a foot-lock you generally give up top position, so only attempt it when you feel the advantage and are sure of your chances of submission. That being said, it pays to emphasize that the simple threat of a foot-lock will make your opponent wary of using positions like the open guard, changing and limiting his fight options.

1 Rodrigo is attempting to pass Shawn's guard. Shawn has his left hand controlling Rodrigo's right sleeve and is using the open guard to keep Rodrigo from passing it. Rodrigo has his right knee up between Shawn's legs to prevent any submission attacks. Rodrigo sees the opportunity for a foot-lock because Shawn's right leg is extended. The first thing Rodrigo wants to do is to trap Shawn's right leg, so he closes his left elbow against his body and presses it onto the top of his own thigh. Rodrigo then starts to lean back and to his left as he slides his left arm along Shawn's right leg, making sure to keep it close to his body, with the elbow maintaining pressure against the thigh.

2 Rodrigo brings his knees together, closing them around Shawn's right leg. Notice that Rodrigo leaves his right knee between Shawn's legs pointing forward to prevent Shawn from scooting closer and sitting up to defend the submission. He places his left foot on Shawn's right hip to prevent him from coming up to defend the foot-lock. Shawn's foot is trapped under Rodrigo's left armpit. Having completely trapped Shawn's right foot, Rodrigo wraps his left arm around the ankle and uses his right hand to give his right lapel to the left hand.

3 Rodrigo grabs the lapel, turns his torso to the left and leans further back. Rodrigo's back will drive Shawn's toes down while the left forearm applies pressure to the Achilles tendon for the foot-lock. It is very important for Rodrigo to turn his body towards the foot that he is attacking to minimize Shawn's chances of escaping the lock.

3 **Detail:** Rodrigo points out the perfect place for his arm to wrap around Shawn's foot. The closer he is to the Achilles and the foot the more leverage he will have when he leans back to extend the foot and apply pressure.

3 **Incorrect:** Make sure you don't let your blocking foot cross over your opponent's stomach instead of pressing against the hip on the same side of the foot being attacked, otherwise you leave yourself open for a heel-hook or a foot-lock counter as Shawn demonstrates here.

Arm-lock from side control: Details

Perfect execution of a submission is always important but it is even more critical in the case of the arm-lock from side control. First, it is always frustrating and at times demoralizing to attempt a submission only to have your opponent escape at the last minute. Second, in the case of the arm-lock, failure to submit means giving up top position and ending up on your back with the opponent in your guard or worse. Rodrigo here gives important and precise details of how to perform the perfect arm-lock from the side control position.

1 Rodrigo is in side control on Shawn's right side. Rodrigo secures control over Shawn's left arm by wrapping his own left arm around it. Rodrigo's left hand grabs the right collar for extra tightness of the grip around the arm. Rodrigo starts to move his body to the north-south position.

2 As he reaches north-south Rodrigo leaves his right knee in front of Shawn's head. This prevents Shawn from spinning his body in a counter-clockwise direction and turning to his left to yank his elbow out of the grip. Rodrigo also already has his right leg on the correct side of Shawn's head for the arm-lock. Rodrigo pulls up on Shawn's left arm, rolling Shawn onto his right side, as he steps forward with his left leg and plants his foot close to Shawn's back to prevent him from turning back and pressing his back flat on the mat. Notice how Rodrigo keeps his hips down so they press on Shawn's shoulder to take away any space for him to pull his arm. By pressing his hips against the back of Shawn's shoulder Rodrigo keeps him from turning to his left to put his back on the mat and yank his elbow away.

3 Rodrigo leans forward as he raises his body so he can plant his right foot in front of Shawn's face. Notice that Rodrigo keeps his chest against Shawn's left arm and drives it towards the right for extra control of the arm. From here Rodrigo sits down and extends his body to complete the arm-lock.

Reverse view from step 2:

2 Rodrigo leans forward with his torso and plants his right arm in front of Shawn's chest between the chest and the arm. Rodrigo's right knee stays on Shawn's right side.

3 Rodrigo pivots off his right arm and leans forward. putting his weight on the right hand with his chest pressing against Shawn's arm. Rodrigo extends his right leg, plants the right foot in front of Shawn's head and raises his left leg so his shin touches Shawn's back with the knee on the ribs. It is very important for Rodrigo to press his body against Shawn's arm for control and to turn him to his side, making a shorter path to reach the proper position to fall for the arm-lock. Remember, it is impossible to apply an arm-lock if you allow the opponent's back to remain flat on the mat. In order to have proper leverage, you must turn him to his side.

3 **Detail:**

Correct: Rodrigo's left elbow is tight against his ribs to eliminate space Shawn could use to pull his arm out.

Incorrect: Rodrigo's left elbow is open and Shawn can easily pull his elbow out, escaping the attack.

4 Rodrigo leans back, extending Shawn's left arm for the arm-lock. Notice that Rodrigo's legs are close together, trapping Shawn's arm and taking away any space for him to pull his elbow out of the lock.

Arm-lock

In the case of the arm-lock the hips need to be tight against the opponent's shoulder and elbow and the legs should be pressing against the arm.

1 Rodrigo attempts an arm-lock on Shawn's right arm. Rodrigo's hips are properly positioned very close to the elbow joint that he is attacking. His pelvis is tight against Shawn's shoulder so that there is no space for Shawn to pull his elbow out and avoid the arm-lock. At the same time this perfectly positions the hips under Shawn's elbow. With this hip placement, Rodrigo not only has the best leverage to pry Shawn's arm open but he also has the hips in position to push against the elbow to hyperextend it for the joint lock. Notice that because of Rodrigo's proper body position, he actually uses his upper body to pull and extend Shawn's arm. He is fighting with the force of his entire upper body against Shawn's arm. The proper mechanics shown here are key to successfully executing an arm-lock against a strong opponent.

2 Rodrigo incorrectly attacks Shawn's right arm for the arm-lock. First and foremost, Rodrigo's hips are far away from Shawn's elbow and shoulder, allowing the space for Shawn to pull the elbow out and escape the arm-lock. Also, since his hips are too distant, the pressure from Rodrigo's hip thrusting up against Shawn's arm would be against the forearm and not the elbow joint. Another incorrect aspect of Rodrigo's attack is his hand position: gripping Shawn's wrist. Rodrigo wants to break Shawn's hands from gripping each other to counter the arm-lock. Because of the hand position, Rodrigo's power is directed toward Shawn's forearm and not the grip. Rodrigo will only be able to pull the forearm in against his stomach and instead of forcing the break of the grip. The proper direction would be for the power to be going up in a semi-circle, applying great pressure on Shawn's handgrip and forcing them to break apart.

3 Correct: Notice Rodrigo's left leg with the knee pressing down against Shawn's chest. This takes away any space for Shawn to attempt an escape. Also notice how Rodrigo's right calf is positioned on top of Shawn's face, pressing down and keeping him from trying to sit up for a stacking attempt.

4 Incorrect: Rodrigo's left knee pointing straight up gives too much space between Rodrigo's shin and Shawn's torso, space that may allow Shawn to try to rotate his body to his left and stack Rodrigo's legs, countering the arm-lock.

Breaking the arm-lock stalemate

Often times when you are able to secure the arm-lock on your opponent, he fiercely defends it by locking his hands or inter-locking the arms, making it hard, especially if he is very strong, for you to break his counter. Rodrigo here demonstrates a few options to deal with the stalemate.

A Opponent grabs his wrist with the opposite hand: Correct

1 Shawn grabs his right wrist with the left hand to defend the arm-lock. Rodrigo grabs his own left collar with the right hand making sure that he wraps Shawn's arm as close to the wrist as possible.

2 Rodrigo leans to his left using the weight of his body to break Shawn's grip and extend the arm while thrusting his hips up against the elbow joint for the arm-lock.

Incorrect:

1 Rodrigo wraps Shawn's right arm with his right arm. This time, however, Rodrigo arm is near Shawn's elbow instead of the wrist.

1 **Correct Detail:** Notice Rodrigo demonstrating that in this case the pressure of the pull is against Shawn's crease of the arm at the elbow. This creates no pressure to extend it, making it very easy for Shawn to keep the arm bent.

2 **Detail:** Rodrigo demonstrates the proper direction of the pressure to break Shawn's locked hands. Notice that he applies pressure in a circular direction to his left to break the stalemate.

B Opponent locks his arms in a figure 4:

1 In this case Shawn defends Rodrigo's arm-lock attempt by grabbing his left biceps with the right hand, bending the left arm to form a figure four by placing the left hand on Rodrigo's thigh.

2 Rodrigo leans forward and slides his right arm up as close to Shawn's right wrist as possible. He then uses his left hand to push Shawn's left wrist back to break the figure 4 lock, freeing the arm.

3 Rodrigo then uses the same motion as in the previous technique to break Shawn's right hand grip on the biceps and extend the arm for the arm-lock.

C Opponent locks his fingers together

(Note: For ease of viewing the technique Rodrigo leaves his left leg open, in a real attempt he would have the leg over Shawn's head.)

1 Shawn locks his fingers together in his attempt to prevent Rodrigo from extending his right arm. This is a weaker grip than both previous ones but still can present a good deal of difficulty. Rodrigo wraps his right arm as close to Shawn's wrist
as possible and places his right foot on top of Shawn's left biceps. Rodrigo then
leans back as he extends his right leg pushing against Shawn's biceps. The force of
Rodrigo's leg pushing forward and his body leaning back will cause Shawn to release
his grip and break the stalemate. Notice that you can use this same option to break
for option A.

Shoulder-lock, or omoplata

For the shoulder-lock, it is important to raise the hips towards the shoulder being attacked and to use the legs and torso to push down and trap the opponent's body.

1 Correct: Rodrigo raises his hips towards Shawn's right shoulder so that the left leg is very close to the shoulder joint where the shoulder-lock is being applied. Rodrigo sits up and turns his body in a clockwise direction, twisting Shawn's arm around in the same direction. Rodrigo pivots around the shoulder, applying torque on the joint for the submission. Notice Rodrigo's body and knee position: to apply the most pressure and for the perfect mechanics the knees are pointing towards Shawn's body and not away from it while his torso leans and presses down on Shawn's back to prevent him from sitting back to escape the pressure.

2 **Incorrect:** Rodrigo tries a "lazy" shoulder lock: he doesn't raise his hips towards the joint, creating a lot of space for Shawn to pull his arm out. Without raising the hips, Rodrigo's left leg is too far from Shawn's shoulder and doesn't apply the proper pressure for the lock. As Rodrigo sits up, his knees and torso point away from Shawn's torso without applying any pressure on Shawn's arm and back, making it very easy for Shawn to raise his torso and kneel back up, defending the shoulder lock.

Key-lock, or Americana

In the key-lock, the elbow needs to be tight against the opponent's head in order to take away any space and to keep the arm bent at the proper angle for the torque around the shoulder.

1 Correct: Rodrigo's left elbow is perpendicular to the ground and tight against Shawn's left ear, his left hand grips around Shawn's left wrist with a claw grip (all five fingers together on the same side). Rodrigo's weight is heavily on his left elbow. The mechanics of the elbow position tight against the ear takes away any space for Shawn to turn his head to his left and escape the attack. Rodrigo's weight on his elbow along with the five fingers together wrapped around the wrist add extra power to the grip, keeping Shawn from being able to extend his arm to defend the key-lock. Notice how Shawn's arm is bent at 90° and not extended past that angle. To finish the attack Rodrigo would wrap his right arm under the left until he locks the right hand on his own left wrist and drag Shawn's left arm down torquing the shoulder.

2 Incorrect: Rodrigo's left elbow is not perpendicular to the ground and is away from Shawn's right ear, so Rodrigo's weight is not on the elbow and Shawn is able to extend the arm taking away Rodrigo's ability to torque it around the shoulder.

40

Kimura

Proper mechanics on the Kimura are similar to the key-lock since the positions mirror each other. The torque applied is on the shoulder, only the direction of the rotation is reversed because the arm points in the opposite direction. Rodrigo's weight and elbow position are keys to maintaining control over the arm and allowing for the best angle for the torque to be applied.

1 Correct: Rodrigo has his right elbow pressing down on the mat next to Shawn's ribs, the arm is perpendicular to the ground. Rodrigo's right hand grips Shawn's left wrist with the claw grip. Rodrigo's left arm wraps under Shawn's arm until the hand grabs his own right wrist. Rodrigo's weight is on his elbows to prevent Shawn from extending the arm. Rodrigo would apply the torque on Shawn's shoulder by dragging Shawn's left wrist on the mat up in the direction of Shawn's left ear, torquing the shoulder.

2 Incorrect: Rodrigo's elbows are away from Shawn and not perpendicular to the ground, so Rodrigo's weight is not pressing them down, allowing Shawn to extend his arm and reduce Rodrigo's ability to torque the arm around the shoulder.

TAKEDOWNS

Gracie Jiu-Jitsu evolves continuously, adapting some of the best moves from other arts to create what is one of the most effective fighting arts there is. Realizing the effectiveness of wrestling in takedown and control situations, a few years ago Jiu-Jitsu borrowed some wrestling moves, especially takedowns.

Most fights and Jiu-Jitsu matches start with the two combatants standing facing each other. While the Gracie Jiu-Jitsu specialist is equally comfortable fighting from the bottom or from the top, most of them prefer to fight from the top. Therefore being able to take your opponent down is a great advantage and a very important part of the complete fighter's arsenal. In the next few pages Rodrigo demonstrates some of the takedowns that he believes are most effective.

The keys to executing a good takedown are to have the control in the battle for the grip (generally the person controlling the middle or the inside has the control) and to initiate a move to take your opponent off-balance and leaning in the direction of your throw. To achieve that you need to execute a feint to have your opponent react by leaning the proper way.

Grip and control power drill 1

In the fight for positional dominance, especially when standing, grips are the key to control the opponent. He who has the control generally wins the immediate battle. It is important then for one to understand the mechanics of grips and control.

Push and pull:

1 The closer your elbows are to your body, the more power you will have. Rodrigo keeps his elbows tight against his body, giving him maximum power.

2 Conversely, the more extended your arms are, the further away from your body your elbows will be, giving you less and less power and control. At the full extension you have very little power, and you do not have the give that the bent arm gives you.

3 In the grip battle, generally speaking, the person whose elbow is closest to his body has the most control. In this case Rodrigo has his left arm bent pulling Shawn's right arm. Rodrigo's elbow is closer to his body than Shawn's elbow is to his own body giving Rodrigo has the control and the advantage here.

4 Shawn now has his elbow closer to his body than Rodrigo so he has the control.

Up and down:

5 Also notice that when the grip is in a different position and the battle is for the up and down movement, the power range is different. In this case Shawn grabs Rodrigo's wrist from above and is pushing instead of pulling. Rodrigo has more power when his arm is extended and the wrist is away from the side of his body. Rodrigo has more power raising his arm than Shawn has when pushing it down. That all changes when Rodrigo's arm is parallel to his body and Shawn's arm is extended. Now Shawn has more power to push Rodrigo's arm than Rodrigo has to defend it. This is extremely important in case of attacks like the kimura and other such situations when understanding the body mechanics can be the difference between fighting a losing battle and gaining power by changing and adjusting your body position. So in the up and down movement the power range is from your body's line up to eye level.

42

Grip and control drill 2

This is one of Rodrigo's favorite grip and control drills. The key to this drill is to begin slowly and feel the situations when you have and when you don't have the control. You and your partner should, in the beginning, allow each other the control until you start to understand at what point of the arm extension control is transferred from you to your opponent. After you have warmed up and started to feel and recognize the control points you both should start to increase the fight, exchanging grips and trying to pull each other off balance. This is a great drill not only to learn about grips and control but also to develop balance in the stand up part of the game.

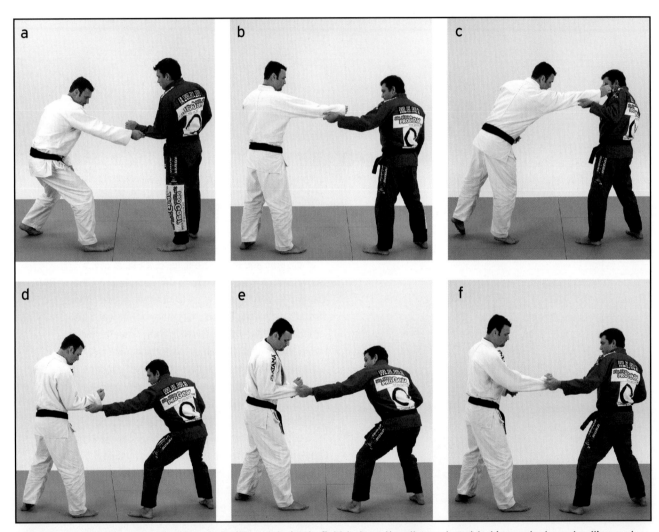

1 Rodrigo and Shawn exchange grip control with each trying to fight to have the elbows closest to his own body, and pulling each other off-balance. Notice Rodrigo's and Shawn's leg position and base, with the hips pointing forward when they are in base and with the torso falling forward when they are not. Notice that when the arm is extended the body follows and balance is lost. But when the elbow is tight and close to your side, the body moves as one, maintaining posture and balance.

Grips and control power drill

Since grip and control are keys to the standing game, this complete drill will greatly improve your skills in those areas. One thing to remember is that the center line is very important in controlling the body. Generally speaking, the person controlling the center line of the opponent's body has the advantage in the control battle.

A Cross side single collar grip

1 Shawn grips Rodrigo's left lapel with his right hand, controlling the center-line. Rodrigo wants to break the grip, so he counters by reaching with his left hand, grabbing Shawn's gi just under the right wrist.

2 Rodrigo then reaches with his right hand and grabs Shawn's right wrist from the side. In one quick jerking motion Rodrigo turns his left shoulder back as he pushes out and to the left with his arms breaking Shawn's grip on the collar.

B Collar and elbow grip

1 Shawn's right hand grips Rodrigo's left collar and the left hand grips Rodrigo's right sleeve under the elbow. Rodrigo first breaks the collar grip in the same way he did with the single collar grip. His left hand holds under Shawn's right wrist and the right hand comes across the wrist. One quick turn of Rodrigo's left shoulder back as he extends the arms breaks Shawn's grip on the collar.

2 Rodrigo continues to grip Shawn's right wrist with his left hand. Shawn pulls his own arm back to release Rodrigo's grip. Rodrigo turns his attention to Shawn's grip on his sleeves. Notice that Rodrigo keeps the right arm bent with the hand in front of his collar to prevent Shawn from grabbing it back again. He then uses the left hand with the arm semi-extended to grab Shawn's left elbow. In a jerking motion Rodrigo turns his right shoulder back and pulls the right arm back, breaking Shawn's grip on the sleeves. Notice that Rodrigo's left arm brace kept Shawn's left elbow in place as he pulled his arm back to break the grip.

C Same side single collar grip:

This time Shawn grabs Rodrigo's on the same side instead of across the body.

1 Shawn uses his right hand to grab Rodrigo's left collar. Notice that this time Rodrigo and Shawn have an open stance with their chests facing the same direction.

2 Rodrigo uses his right hand to open Shawn's collar as he reaches under Shawn's right arm with his left arm and grabs the collar as high as possible. Rodrigo raises his left elbow, lifting Shawn's right arm. Notice that now Rodrigo has the inside position with his left arm under Shawn's right arm taking away some of Shawn's ability to control the collar. Rodrigo then grabs his own left collar with the right hand and yanks it back as he quickly turns his right shoulder back, breaking Shawn's grip on the collar.

D Sleeve and collar grip:

Now Shawn controls Rodrigo's left collar with the right hand and Rodrigo's right sleeve with his left hand. Both fighters are in an open stance.

1 Rodrigo deals with the sleeve grip. Rodrigo uses a straight left arm to keep Shawn away and leans back, placing the weight of his body on the right leg. Rodrigo coils his left leg so the left knee goes right above Shawn's left wrist. In one movement Rodrigo drives the left knee down against Shawn's wrist as he yanks his right arm back, breaking Shawn's grip. Rodrigo can break the collar grip in the same manner as he did in the prior technique (technique C).

E Sleeve grip

1 Shawn controls Rodrigo's right sleeve above the wrist. Rodrigo circles his right hand around Shawn's left until he has his hand under Shawn's wrist and the wrist is turned and facing up.

2 Rodrigo places his left hand on Shawn's left elbow using a stiff arm to keep the elbow in place. In one quick motion Rodrigo yanks his right arm back breaking Shawn's grip.

F Collar and elbow grip: Opponent leans back 1:

In this case Shawn has Rodrigo's left collar and right sleeve and he is leaning back, making it harder for Rodrigo to use technique B.

1 Shawn holds Rodrigo's left collar with the right hand and the left sleeve at the elbow with his left hand as he leans back keeping distance from Rodrigo. Rodrigo twists his torso to the right, forcing Shawn to lean forward to maintain the grip. Rodrigo then circles his left hand under Shawn's right arm. Notice Rodrigo's left arm is bent at the elbow and shoots straight up to break Shawn's control.

2 Rodrigo's left hand grabs the back of Shawn's right shoulder. He then circles his right hand around the top of Shawn's left arm and grabs the sleeve at the elbow, countering Shawn's control.

2 Reverse: Notice Rodrigo's left arm position: the arm is bent at the elbow at 90° and the forearm braces against Shawn's right shoulder to maintain distance.

G Collar and elbow grip: Opponent leans back 2:
Another solid option to break the collar and elbow grip when the opponent leans back is shown here.

1 Shawn holds Rodrigo's left collar with the right hand and the left sleeve at the elbow with his left hand as he leans back, keeping distance from Rodrigo. Rodrigo twists his torso to the left, forcing Shawn to lean forward to maintain the grip, and raises his left arm high.

2 Pivoting on his feet, Rodrigo turns his body back to his right as he circles the left arm over the top of Shawn's right arm while dropping the elbow straight down in front of Shawn's arm. Notice Rodrigo's weight changed to his right leg and his upper body leans forward to add weight to the left elbow.

3 Rodrigo wraps the left arm around Shawn's back and grabs the belt. He steps in closer to Shawn, placing his left foot next to Shawn's right foot. He then steps in front of Shawn with the left foot so his hips are square in front of Shawn's hips and executes the hip throw.

H Belt grip:

In the event the opponent holds your belt, he has great advantage and control over you. You must quickly counter by getting inside control by holding his belt.

1 Shawn has his left hand controlling Rodrigo's belt. Notice Shawn and Rodrigo's stance is open with their hips facing in the same direction.

2 Rodrigo quickly pivots on his right foot, turning his body slightly to the left. He slides his right arm between Shawn's left arm and body until his hand grabs the back of Shawn's belt. Rodrigo pulls up on the belt as he continues to twist his body to the left. From here Rodrigo can execute many throws such as the hip throw or the uchimata.

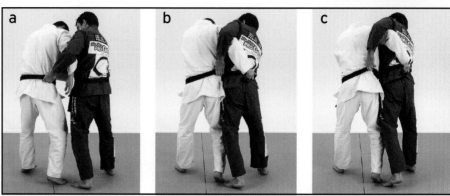

I Countering the supplex:

The supplex is a devastating wrestling takedown as the person getting thrown is hoisted over the top of the thrower landing on the back of his head and shoulders. It is therefore very important to know a simple counter to it.

1 As Shawn tries to execute a supplex, he wraps his arms around Rodrigo's waist, locking the hands in front. He bends his legs and starts to explosively extend the legs as he throws Rodrigo over his shoulder. Rodrigo counters by quickly wrapping his right foot around Shawn's right leg, impeding him from executing the throw.

1 **Side view:** For the supplex to work there needs to be space between the legs of the two fighters as the thrower bends and hoists his opponent backwards. Notice how Rodrigo grapevines his right leg around Shawn's right leg, preventing Shawn's ability to hoist Rodrigo over his head by keeping his legs connected with Shawn's.

Hip throw drill

The hip throw is one of the most basic and most important throws in Gracie Jiu-Jitsu. It is used in many self-defense techniques and is a devastating throw and a fight ender when properly executed. The opponent gets thrown with great amplitude over the back of the attacker, landing on his back.

1 Rodrigo stands next to Shawn. His right arm is wrapped under Shawn's left arm with his hand holding Shawn's belt near the right side. Rodrigo and Shawn walk forward, both taking a step with the outside leg – Rodrigo's left and Shawn's right.

2 Rodrigo and Shawn may take two sets of steps or start the drill on the first one. As Shawn continues to walk forward, taking a step with the right leg, Rodrigo steps in front of Shawn with his right leg. Rodrigo turns his hips to the right as he bends the knees so he can lock his hips right in front of Shawn's hips while he uses his right arm to pull up Shawn's belt. Rodrigo drops his head towards the mat and extends his legs as he bends forward and pulls Shawn's body by the belt, lifting him of the mat in the hip throw motion. Notice that in the drill Rodrigo does not complete the hip throw sending Shawn over the top of his back. Instead, he straightens his body, lets Shawn back on the ground, and they start walking side by side again for the next throw set up. Repeat the drill from the other side.

Takedown 1: Outside trip

In the outside trip (in Judo, this move is named *Osotogari*), Rodrigo tricks Shawn into putting his weight on one foot and attacks the other side with a trip to complete the takedown.

1 Rodrigo's left hand grabs Shawn's right sleeve under the elbow while his right hand grabs Shawn's left collar. Shawn has the reverse grip so there is no grip advantage. The fighters are facing each other.

2 Rodrigo initiates the attack by raising his left arm, driving Shawn's right elbow up while pulling down Shawn's left collar with his right arm. This forces Shawn to lean to his left and place more of his weight on the left leg, leaving the right leg light. Shawn reacts to the move by trying to re-steady his body and center his weight.

3 Taking advantage of Shawn's reaction, Rodrigo takes a step forward with his left leg so his foot lands on the outside next to or past Shawn's right foot. Rodrigo leans forward, putting his weight on his left foot. He drives his right stiff arm on Shawn's chest, forcing Shawn to lean back, while pulling down on the right arm with his left hand. Notice how Shawn is off-balance with his weight on the right leg and falling back to his right.

3 Reverse: Notice Rodrigo's right arm is pushing Shawn's left shoulder while the left arm pulls down on Shawn's right sleeve, forcing his torso to the right and back.

4 Rodrigo lightly raises his right leg and swings it forward past Shawn's right leg and then kicks it back between Shawn's legs, clipping Shawn's right leg back with his thigh. At the same time Rodrigo drives his right hand forward, pushing Shawn's chest back, and pulls down hard on Shawn's right sleeve with his left hand, forcing Shawn to go flying into the takedown. Notice that for the perfect move, the tips of Rodrigo's toes lightly kick the mat as they pass next to Shawn's right foot on the return motion.

Takedown 2: Leg pick

In the leg pick Rodrigo first forces Shawn to step forward, putting his weight on the right foot. Shawn's reaction is to resist. Rodrigo takes advantage of that and pulls Shawn forward so he steps for-

ward with the left leg, putting his weight on that leg, as Rodrigo grabs and pulls up on the right leg for the takedown.

1 Rodrigo has grip control with his left hand controlling Shawn's right collar. His left elbow is raised to deflect Shawn's right arm which has control of Rodrigo's left shoulder. Rodrigo's right hand grabs Shawn's left wrist to prevent him from gaining a grip.

2 Rodrigo changes his right hand's position to grab Shawn's left collar and pulls him forward, forcing Shawn to step forward with his right leg.

3 Rodrigo continues to pull Shawn forward while twisting his upper body. He uses his right hand to pull down on the left collar and the left hand to twist up on the left collar while pulling forward. Shawn has to take a step forward with his left foot to gain balance. Rodrigo continues to drive Shawn forward and to his left with his right hand as he lets go of the right collar. His left hand is now free to quickly reach and grab the back of Shawn's right thigh, lifting it up. Notice that Shawn's right leg was in range because Rodrigo had previously forced him to step forward.

4 Rodrigo continues to pull up on Shawn's right leg while driving his left side down with his right hand as he steps forward with his left leg, turning and driving Shawn to the ground for the takedown.

Takedown 3: Duck under takedown variation

The duck under takedown is one of wrestling's premier takedowns and Shawn demonstrates a variation here in which rather than wrapping both legs with his arms, he instead uses the grip on the gi on one side.

1 To execute the best duck under Shawn wants Rodrigo to be leaning forward with his weight on his front leg, so Shawn sets up the duck under with a front foot step on Rodrigo's front foot. In a battle for grip control Shawn ends up with his left hand controlling Rodrigo's right sleeve and his right hand on Rodrigo's left shoulder. Rodrigo has his left foot forward and Shawn the right. Shawn twists Rodrigo's torso to the right while stepping with his right foot on top of Rodrigo's left foot in an attempt to trip Rodrigo.

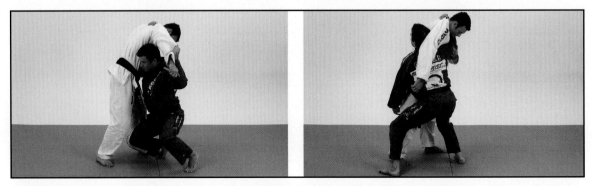

2 While still pulling Rodrigo's torso forward with his hands, Shawn quickly drops down by bending the knees. He slides his head under Rodrigo's right arm, locking his right shoulder under the armpit, and wraps his left hand around the back of Rodrigo's right leg. In the same motion, Shawn pushes off his legs, lifting Rodrigo off the mat. Notice that Shawn keeps his back straight when lifting Rodrigo, using only his legs to lift and not his back. Otherwise he may injure his back.

3 Shawn continues the takedown by extending his legs in an explosive motion while lifting Rodrigo by the left shoulder and right leg. At the height of his lift, Shawn pulls down on Rodrigo's shoulder with the right hand while he continues to lift Rodrigo's right leg with his left hand. This turns Rodrigo's body completely around. Shawn drops him to the mat on his back.

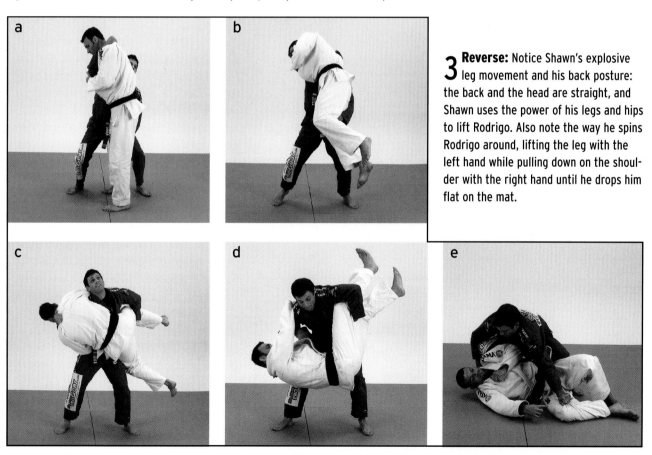

3 Reverse: Notice Shawn's explosive leg movement and his back posture: the back and the head are straight, and Shawn uses the power of his legs and hips to lift Rodrigo. Also note the way he spins Rodrigo around, lifting the leg with the left hand while pulling down on the shoulder with the right hand until he drops him flat on the mat.

48

Counter to the rear clinch: Kimura

The rear bear hug is a dangerous position to be caught in. From there, unless you counter it properly, only bad things can happen. One very effective way to counter the rear bear hug is to apply the kimura. The kimura is generally applied on the arm whose hand is on top clinching. The key to this counter is to be able to pry the opponent's hands apart and bring him to the ground into the guard. You may attempt to crank the opponent's arm around to his ear without placing him in the guard, but if you don't have complete control he may be able to walk around and counter, or simply go with the movement and circle around to avoid the submission pressure.

1 Shawn has a rear clinch on Rodrigo. Since his right hand is on top of the left, Rodrigo will attack that arm. First he needs to break Shawn's lock with his hands clasped together, so he begins by grabbing Shawn's right wrist with his left hand and driving it out as he steps forward with his left foot. This opens the space for his right arm to wrap around Shawn's right arm. Notice that Rodrigo's right arm must come in above Shawn's right elbow, in order to lock the elbow and have the proper hold for the kimura.

2 Once he locks his right hand onto his own left wrist, completing the kimura lock around Shawn's right arm, Rodrigo steps further forward with his left leg. Rodrigo then cocks his right leg, bringing the heel up, and places his shin in front of Shawn's hips. He hooks his right foot outside Shawn's hips. He cranks the kimura, driving Shawn's arm in a clockwise direction, to break the hand grip.

3 Rodrigo hops to his left on his left foot, squaring his hips, and faces Shawn. Rodrigo's right leg naturally turns and ends up on the outside of Shawn's left hip. He then bends his left knee until his back is on the mat. Because Rodrigo's right foot was hooked on the outside of Shawn's left hip, and his left leg is slightly outside of Shawn's right leg, Shawn ends up between Rodrigo's legs in the guard. Notice that as he does this move, Rodrigo is already torquing Shawn's arm. Rodrigo slides his body out to his left and turns on to his right side, always keeping his left leg on Shawn's back, preventing him from rolling forward and over his right shoulder to escape the shoulder lock.

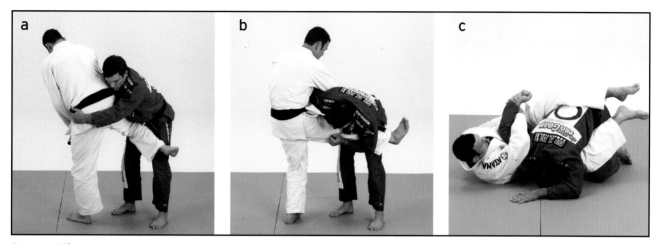

Reverse View:

Notice how Rodrigo has cocked his right leg, using the shin in front of Shawn's hips to keep distance and hooks the foot on Shawn's hip to prevent him from circling around to Rodrigo's back. This also makes him end up inside the guard as Rodrigo goes to the mat. Notice how Rodrigo's right leg position, with the heel locked against Shawn's left thigh, prevents him from circling up to reach Rodrigo's side and to avoid the kimura.

Details:

Correct: Rodrigo presses his right elbow down against Shawn's shoulder while keeping Shawn's elbow tight against his chest to prevent Shawn from extending the arm and from raising his right shoulder.

Incorrect: Rodrigo doesn't press down on Shawn's shoulder with his elbow, allowing Shawn to extend the arm and defend the kimura.

GUARD DEFENSE BASICS

Another key aspect of Gracie Jiu-Jitsu is defending the guard. Although there are lots of different techniques that are used to defend the guard, there are some solid basic principles that apply in any situation.

FIGURE 1

FIGURE 2

- Don't let your opponent control your hips

- Don't let your opponent control both your legs: Your legs are the front line barriers to stop your opponent from passing your guard. If your opponent is able to control both of your legs he has gained a huge advantage and is half way to passing your guard. Always try to break his control of your legs early by breaking his hand grips (see figure 1).

- Don't let your opponent put your back on the ground: Being able to move your hips and torso allow you to alter the dynamics of the position, deflect your opponent's power and redirect his weight and pressure. By allowing him to put your back on the ground, you severely limit your ability to escape your hips and move your body (see figure 1).

- Don't let your opponent get past the imaginary line in front of your knees (figures 2 and 3): Your foot, shin and knee form one of the most effective tools to block your opponent's progress in passing your guard. By constantly and continuously using them to block your opponent's body and hips you are not only able to stop his progress but also frustrate him. Once he gets past that line (figure 4) then he has broken past your guard barrier and you need to replace and recoup.

FIGURE 3

FIGURE 4

Examples:

Pass the imaginary line

At this point Rodrigo still has control of the position, as Shawn has not passed the imaginary line in front of his knee.

Shawn breaks past that line and is now in good position to pass Rodrigo's guard. Notice Rodrigo shows the line with his right hand.

Rodrigo is still back from Shawn's knee line.

Rodrigo has passed Shawn's knee line and is now on the thigh line having passed the guard.

Keep your knees pointing out:
Rodrigo's knees are pointing out and act as barriers Shawn must pass (figure A).
Rodrigo's knees are closed together making it easy for Shawn to control Rodrigo's legs and pass his guard (figure B).

Always remain connected to your opponent:

It is important to remain connected with your opponent, otherwise he has the freedom to move around you. Maintain control of his body at all times, either by controlling his arms or his arm and one leg.

Notice Shawn breaking two rules. First, Shawn is not connected with Rodrigo. Second, Rodrigo controls both of Shawn's legs and is able to easily pass his guard by stepping around them.

Shawn remains connected with Rodrigo by grapevining his legs around Rodrigo's arms.

Always keep your legs slightly coiled so you have some power left. Once you fully extend your legs you have no more power left in reserve.

Rodrigo's legs are fully extended and he can no longer press against Shawn's biceps, allowing Shawn to free his arms and push Rodrigo's legs down to the mat.

The defender generally is in control of which side the opponent attempts his pass. For instance, if Rodrigo puts his right leg out and turns to his left, he makes it very difficult for Shawn to pass towards his right side. Therefore he forces Shawn to try passing to the left.

Guard replacement drill

As we stated earlier, replacing the guard is a key skill if you hope to be a successful Gracie Jiu-Jitsu fighter. In this drill Rodrigo practices replacing and defending the guard, while at the same time Shawn practices passing the guard and changing sides. This drill trains Rodrigo's hip escape, his leg-blocking defense for the guard and Shawn's ability to switch sides when passing the guard.

1 Shawn has side-control on Rodrigo's right side. Rodrigo has his left hand resting on Shawn's left shoulder with the forearm pressing against his throat.

2 Rodrigo initiates the drill with the hip escape. He plants his left foot out and pushes off it to turn his body to his right while using the forearm against Shawn's throat to create a barrier. At the same time Rodrigo curls his right leg, sliding the knee in front of Shawn's hips until he can hook his right foot on Shawn's right hip. Rodrigo then loops the left leg over Shawn's head until it is all the way over Shawn's left shoulder, locking the calf on the left arm. Rodrigo has effectively blocked Shawn's ability to pass to Rodrigo's right.

3 Shawn's part of the drill begins here: he props his hips up as he extends his legs and pushes off his feet. Shawn drives his left shoulder on top of Rodrigo's left thigh, pushing it down to pin Rodrigo's hips, and plants the left hand on the mat with the arm between Rodrigo's legs. Shawn grabs Rodrigo's right ankle with his right hand and pushes it down, freeing the hook and allowing him to move to his own right to pass Rodrigo's guard in that direction. Shawn steps across with his left leg under the right, making sure he pins Rodrigo's right ankle to the mat with his right arm. Once he clears Rodrigo's hips, Shawn kneels down with the left knee next to Rodrigo's hips. Shawn steps over with his right leg and tries to reach side control on Rodrigo's left side, aiming to grab Rodrigo's head with his right arm.

4 Rodrigo returns to his drill; as soon as he sees Shawn nearing his left side, he turns his body to his left and does his part of the drill over again. Rodrigo and Shawn can continue with the drill over and over until they decide to change to another drill.

Power and control: Defending and passing the guard

In the guard situation, power and control are defined by who controls the legs and hips and whether or not the block is effective. In most cases, if the person on top is able to deflect the leg block he has a definite advantage in controlling the pass, whereas if the fighter on the bottom is able to use his legs effectively to block the opponent's progress, he gains the advantage in defending the guard.

1 Shawn is attempting to pass Rodrigo's guard. He is able to grip Rodrigo's left leg with his right hand and is pushing it down, driving it between his legs. In this case Shawn has a definite advantage as he has effectively removed Rodrigo's ability to use one of his legs to block Shawn's pass attempt.

2 Now, although Shawn has similar control over Rodrigo's left leg, Rodrigo is able to place his left foot on Shawn's right hip. The foot blocks Shawn's hips from advancing, stopping Shawn's pass attempt. Rodrigo can push off his foot, extending his legs and driving Shawn's body away from his. Now Shawn's weight is on the mat and not on top of Rodrigo's hips, so not only is Shawn slightly off-balance but also Rodrigo's hips are free to move in and out and side to side. Rodrigo has the definite advantage here.

3 Shawn is able to advance in his pass attempt but Rodrigo manages to place his left hand on Shawn's right hip using the stiff left arm as a block to Shawn's advance. As long as the situation remains the same Rodrigo has regained the control and advantage of the situation. For Shawn to further advance in his pass attempt he needs to remove Rodrigo's right arm block. He may do it in several ways: pushing Rodrigo's elbow down and buckling the arm, or pulling Rodrigo's wrist up and removing the hand from his hips. Notice that Rodrigo reacts quickly enough to the situation to be able to use the straight arm to block. If Rodrigo doesn't react as quickly he has to use the bent arm with the forearm acting as the block. This is not as good a block as it allows Shawn to get closer to him.

4 Another very powerful option for Rodrigo to block Shawn's advance is for Rodrigo to place his left hand on Shawn's right hip. This time instead of keeping the left arm straight, he bends it and places the elbow on the mat. By using the proper angle, as shown here, Rodrigo's arm transfers Shawn's weight and forward pressure straight to the mat, allowing Rodrigo to rest while defending the position.

5 Another way to block and gain control is for Rodrigo to use his left arm bent at 90° with the elbow touching his left knee. By keeping the elbow connected with the knee Rodrigo effectively creates another very strong barrier against Shawn's passing attempt. As long as the elbow and knee are tight and connected, even when Shawn tries to pull the elbow up to remove the block, he actually helps bring Rodrigo's left knee and shin in front of his hips and the block gets stronger.

Guard defense drill 1: Open guard hooks

To successfully defend the open guard you need to able to use your feet as hooks. This will help you counter your opponent's ability to move around your legs and also to control your hips and your legs. Rodrigo here demonstrates a series of five drills that can be done as a single sequence or as individual drills. The main objective of these drills is to simply keep your legs and feet hooking and stopping your opponent's attempts to control your body.

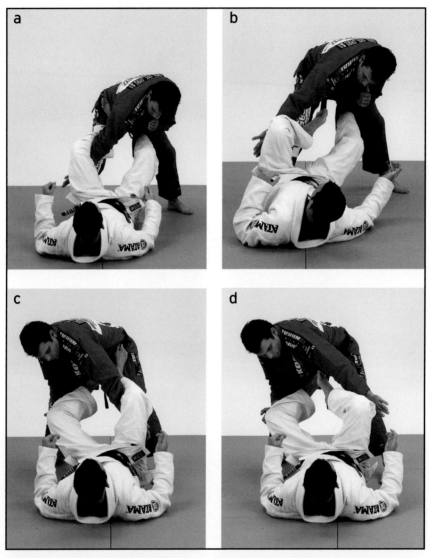

1 Shawn stands in front of Rodrigo, who has his feet on Shawn's hips. Shawn underhooks Rodrigo's left leg with his right arm. Rodrigo turns his torso to his right and circles the leg around the top of Shawn's right arm. As soon as he feels the release of his right arm Shawn uses the left arm to underhook Rodrigo's right leg, Rodrigo then turns his torso to his left and loops his right leg around the top of Shawn's left arm. Do this as a continuous motion drill: as Shawn moves from one side to the other, Rodrigo underhooks first one side then, as Shawn moves to the other side, Rodrigo switches and underhooks the other.

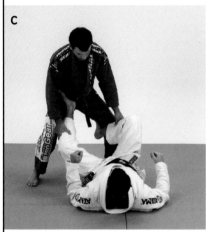

2 Shawn stands in front of Rodrigo with his hands touching Rodrigo's shins. Rodrigo has his feet on Shawn's hips. Shawn steps to his right driving Rodrigo's legs in the same direction. Rodrigo loops his right foot around Shawn's left leg, hooking the foot under the thigh just above the knee. With this hook Rodrigo stops Shawn from being able to walk to the right and around his legs, as the hook will continuously pull Rodrigo's body around keeping him in front of Shawn. Shawn steps back to the left and centers his body with Rodrigo's. Rodrigo releases the hook and places his feet once again on Shawn's hips. Shawn then goes to his left as he tries to circle around Rodrigo's legs. Rodrigo loops the left leg around Shawn's right leg, hooking the foot under the thigh just above the knee. Notice that the direction of Shawn's movement dictates which foot Rodrigo needs to hook – it is always the foot farthest from the direction of the movement. Another way to look at it so you can easily react is you always hook the leg that stays back. If he moves the right leg, he is moving toward the right so the left leg stays behind.

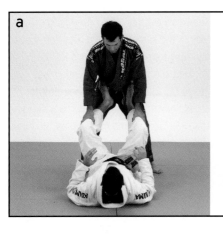

3 Starting from the same initial position, this time Shawn steps back and to the left with his left leg as he pushes Rodrigo's left foot off his hips and drives it down. Rodrigo pushes off his right leg, loops the left leg over and around Shawn's right thigh until he locks the hook and turns his torso to the right to face Shawn's hips. Shawn repeats the move to the opposite side with Rodrigo pushing off the left leg, looping the right foot around and over Shawn's left thigh until he hooks the foot under and brings his torso to his left to face Shawn.

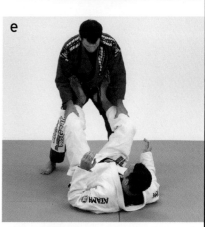

4 Rodrigo starts with Shawn standing in front of him with a typical open guard control. Rodrigo has his right foot pushing on Shawn's left biceps and his left foot pushing on Shawn's right hip. While his right hand grips Shawn's right collar the left grips Shawn's right sleeve at the elbow. Shawn circles his left arm under Rodrigo's right leg, but Rodrigo quickly replaces the foot pushing up on Shawn's left biceps.

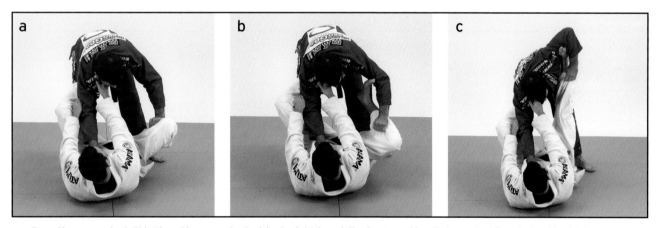

5 From the same start, this time Shawn grabs Rodrigo's right leg at the knee pushing it down. Rodrigo circles his right leg under Shawn's left forearm until he can replace the foot on the biceps and extends the leg to push the arm away.

Guard defense drill 2: Closed guard to open guard

In this drill Rodrigo practices several things: hip movement, using his legs to move his body and transitioning from the closed guard to the open guard. This drill is particularly important because many times in a match you have to quickly transition between different guard postures in reaction to your opponent's actions.

1 Rodrigo has Shawn in his closed guard. He holds Shawn's right collar with his right hand and Shawn's right elbow with the left.

2 The first transition is to the left side: Rodrigo opens the legs, plants the right foot on the mat and pushes off it to escape his hips to the right. Rodrigo turns his body to the left and slides the right knee in front of Shawn's hips until he has his shin in front of the hips with the right foot hooked on Shawn's left side of the hip.

3 Rodrigo's left leg opens up slightly to allow his body the room to turn to the left. Once he is on his side Rodrigo curls the left leg in and places the sole of his foot on Shawn's right hip. Rodrigo then straightens his body, pulling Shawn forward and off-balance, creating space for his right leg to curl. He slides the knee in front of Shawn's chest just under the arm and places his right foot on Shawn's left hip. Rodrigo pushes off his legs and moves his hips further away from Shawn and turns his hips and body back to center, facing Shawn.

4 The second transition is to the right: Rodrigo wraps his legs back around Shawn's body and closes the guard again. Rodrigo then changes his hand grip, reaching for Shawn's left collar with the left hand and Shawn's left sleeve at the elbows with the right hand.

5 Rodrigo repeats the move to the right: he opens the legs, plants the left foot on the mat, pushing off it to escape the hips to the left. He then slides the left knee in front of Shawn's hips, puts the right foot on Shawn's left hip and pushes off it to move his body further away from Shawn's. Rodrigo then curls the left leg and slides the left knee in front of Shawn's chest, placing the left foot on Shawn's right hip. Rodrigo pushes off his feet and re-centers his body with Shawn's while pulling him forward and off-balance. Rodrigo slides the feet off Shawn's hips, wraps the legs around his body and locks his feet to go back to the closed guard.

53

Guard defense drill 3: Cross over sweep

This drill not only replicates the cross over sweep but it also works your abdominal muscles and your ability to sit up. Many times in defending the guard you are forced to sit up – to counter your opponent pinning your legs in a toreana pass or so you can transition to a butterfly guard – and this drill will get your sitting motion extremely sharp.

1 Rodrigo has Shawn in his closed guard. He unlocks his legs and places both feet on the ground next to Shawn's legs.

2 Rodrigo turns his torso to the right as he opens the right arm out so his elbow is next to his head. Pushing off the elbow and using the momentum from rotation of his body Rodrigo starts to sit up. Rodrigo continues rising up as he drops the right leg down slightly and rolls up on the right arm until he is pushing off his hand. Rodrigo twists his body to the right, swinging his left arm, crossing over Shawn's head to help prop him up. Rodrigo wraps his left arm around Shawn's left arm as if he was going to do a cross over sweep.

3 Rodrigo drops his body back down with the arms straight back and repeats the motion in the opposite direction.

Guard defense drill 4: Leg and body swing

Being able to turn your body from one side to the other is a valuable tool in Gracie Jiu-Jitsu, as transitioning from one side to another will often open up different opportunities for attacks – and for escapes as well. In this case Rodrigo drills two different areas at the same time: first, using your arm swing to move your upper body from one side to the other, and second, using your legs to push against the opponent's side to move your hips and your body (an often overlooked ability). These are especially important in guard defense so practice them frequently.

1 Rodrigo starts out with his legs open and the arms held straight back over the head. Rodrigo pushes the back of his left thigh against Shawn's right thigh and uses it to turns his body to the right. At the same time Rodrigo swings the arms forward, using the momentum to bring his torso to the right and closer to Shawn's body. Notice how Rodrigo uses pushing the back of his legs against Shawn to move his body: he pushes the back of his left thigh to turn his body to the right and then pushes his right leg against Shawn's side to help pull his torso forward.

2 Rodrigo swings his arms back and pushes off the back of his right leg and the front of his left to bring his torso back to center. Rodrigo then repeats the move to the opposite side.

Arm-lock from the guard

The arm-lock from the guard is another one of the basic moves that make Gracie Jiu-Jitsu such an effective art. The ability to submit someone when fighting with your back on the ground is one of the tenets of the art and the arm-lock from the guard constitutes one of its pillars. Even though the technique is widely used and easily recognized, it is still a feared and effective submission, especially when used in combination with other submissions or sweeps. The key to the arm-lock from the guard is hip movement and arm control.

1 Rodrigo has Shawn in his closed guard. With his left hand he controls Shawn's right wrist at the sleeve. He circles his right arm under Shawn's left arm until he can grab Shawn's right triceps just above the elbow. With this grip Rodrigo secures control over Shawn's right arm and is ready to proceed with the arm-lock.

1 **Incorrect:** Rodrigo reaches with the right arm over Shawn's left arm trying to grab Shawn's right elbow. All Shawn needs to do is to raise his left elbow and he will block Rodrigo from reaching his right arm.

2 Rodrigo opens the guard by unlocking his feet, and places his left foot either on the ground or on Shawn's right hip. He pushes off it to escape his hips to the left while turning his torso to the right. At the same time he raises his right leg up so that it locks right under Shawn's left armpit. Rodrigo's calf presses down on Shawn's shoulder to prevent him from pulling his torso away.

3 Having secured control over Shawn's torso Rodrigo now braces his left hand against Shawn's left shoulder and places the forearm in front of Shawn's face. Rodrigo's forearm keeps Shawn from leaning in with his head and torso. This creates the perfect distance for Rodrigo to loop his left leg over Shawn's head for the arm-lock. Rodrigo uses both arms to grab Shawn's wrist as he extends his hips up, pressing against Shawn's elbow and hyperextending it for the arm-lock.

3 Incorrect: Rodrigo uses the palm of his hand on Shawn's face to maintain the distance. His arm is not strong enough to keep Shawn from leaning against the hand and buckles at the elbow. Notice that when done correctly – using the forearm to block – Rodrigo does not have to exert any power to keep Shawn's head and torso away.

Toreana guard pass defense

One of the most common and effective ways to pass the guard when standing is to use the toreana or bull fighter's guard pass method. In this method the passer controls both the defender's legs and simply steps around them to reach side control. Rodrigo here demonstrates a couple of defenses to the pass.

A

1 Rodrigo has Shawn in his open guard. He is connected with his right foot pushing against Shawn's arm.

2 Shawn pushes Rodrigo's left leg down with his right arm and steps back to release Rodrigo's foot from his left arm. At this point Shawn has regained control and starts to push Rodrigo's legs to the ground to start the toreana pass.

3 Rodrigo immediately sits up and wraps both his hands on the outside of Shawn's arms gripping behind the triceps to keeping him from walking around Rodrigo's legs for the pass.

B

1 Shawn gains control of Rodrigo's legs, as he is able to step back while grabbing Rodrigo's gi pants. Notice that at this point Rodrigo's legs are extended and not exerting any pressure against Shawn's arms. If Rodrigo doesn't react, Shawn will push them towards the mat and pass his guard with the toreana pass.

2 Rodrigo quickly loops his left leg over the top of Shawn's right arm until he can hook his foot under the arm to regain control.

3 Rodrigo then spins his torso to the right to further hook his foot and to pull Shawn's body off-balance, causing Shawn to fall on top of him. Notice that Rodrigo keeps control over Shawn's arms with his hands gripping the sleeves at all times. Otherwise Shawn can simply move his arm over the leg and regain the control of the position.

Breaking the opponent's posture: Arm-wrap: Opponent blocks arm

As previously stated, breaking the opponent's posture involves breaking his grip and attacking the forward arm. In this case Rodrigo does both with the arm wrap

1 Rodrigo has Shawn in his closed guard. He has his right hand inside Shawn's collar ready to attack with a choke. Shawn counters the move with his own right hand blocking Rodrigo's left biceps, preventing Rodrigo from easily reaching the opposite collar to apply the choke. Rodrigo circles his left hand under Shawn's right forearm.

2 Using his legs to help pivot his body to his right Rodrigo shoots his left arm under Shawn's elbow and towards his own head as if he wants to comb his own hair. By doing this Rodrigo breaks Shawn's right arm brace and breaks his posture.

3 Rodrigo wraps his left arm around Shawn's right arm to complete the arm-wrap. Notice that Rodrigo opens his legs to help move his hips out to the left and then closes them again once he has the arm wrap to regain full closed guard.

Closed guard

The closed guard is the staple of the guard. In it, your opponent is contained between your legs and you have full control over him until such time as he is able to gain posture, forcing you to change to the open guard. A variety of chokes and arm-locks work from the closed guard so long as you are able to keep your opponent at the proper distance and not allow him to gain posture. The keys to breaking posture are:

➤ Attack the opponent's front arm (the one he places on your chest to maintain his distance).

➤ Use your legs and hips to push and pull your opponent's torso.

➤ Try to prevent your opponent from gaining solid grips on your gi.

➤ If possible control his head by grabbing it with one of your hands.

58

Breaking the opponent's posture: Arm wrap: Opponent grabs collar

At times your opponent will have a stronger grip with his posturing (front) hand. In this case Shawn grips Rodrigo's collar with his right hand to prevent Rodrigo from easily breaking his grip. Notice that Shawn's his left hand grips Rodrigo's belt and presses it down to the mat to prevent Rodrigo from easily being able to move his hips. Since Shawn has a better grip than in the previous situation Rodrigo uses a different way to break the grip and reach the arm wrap.

1 Rodrigo has Shawn in the closed guard. Shawn's left hand presses down on Rodrigo's belt to pin the hips to the mat while his right hand grabs Rodrigo's collar at the chest to maintain distance and posture.

2 Rodrigo turns his torso to the left while using his right hand to grab Shawn's right sleeve wrist, making sure that his elbow is above his own head. At the same time Rodrigo slides his left arm under Shawn's right forearm to help break the grip.

3 Rodrigo shoots his left arm through the gap between his torso and Shawn's right forearm while he pulls up on the sleeve with his right hand to break the grip. Notice how Rodrigo turns his torso to the right so he can add the power of his entire body to help break Shawn's grip on his collar.

4 Rodrigo continues pulling up on Shawn's right sleeve with his right arm forcing Shawn to fall forward. At the same time Rodrigo wraps his left arm around Shawn's right arm.

5 Rodrigo uses his legs to help move his hips to the left so he can use his left hand to grip Shawn's left collar and complete the arm wrap control over Shawn's right arm. Once he does that he closes his legs back for closed guard. Notice that as he turns his hips to the left Rodrigo has the makings of an armbar on Shawn's right arm. Should he decide to attack it all he has to do is arch his torso back and to the left to extend Shawn's right arm, and bend his left leg placing the knee on top of Shawn's right elbow to break it.

Guard defense: Creating space and preventing your opponent from controlling your head

One of the keys to preventing your opponent from passing your guard is for you to be able to create distance. This keeps him from pressing so tight with his chest on your chest that he can control your upper body. It also prevents him from controlling your head by wrapping his arm around it. Rodrigo demonstrates a few options to achieve these objectives.

Correct:

1 As Shawn tries to pass Rodrigo's guard, he reaches half-guard on the right side. Rodrigo uses his right hand to cup Shawn's left biceps to prevent him from wrapping that arm around Rodrigo's head. Should Rodrigo fail to stop Shawn's left arm from wrapping around his head, he will give Shawn control over his head and upper body making it very hard for him to prevent Shawn from passing his guard and reaching side control.

2 While still using his right hand to block Shawn's left arm from wrapping his head, Rodrigo wants to create space between his chest and Shawn's. He slides his left arm between their chests so that the left hand rests on Shawn's left shoulder and the forearm is in front of Shawn's throat. By bracing on his left hand and raising his elbow Rodrigo drives his left forearm on Shawn's Adam's apple forcing him to move his torso back and creating space between their chests. Rodrigo will use that space to move his body in a direction so he can replace the guard.

Incorrect:

1 Rodrigo tries to block Shawn's pass by using his right hand to block Shawn's left hip to prevent him from reaching his side.

2 With his left arm free, Shawn quickly wraps it around Rodrigo's head and gains great control over his upper body.

3 Shawn turns his hips in a clockwise direction, breaking the right hand brace that was ineffective in stopping his advance. Most important, in the event that Shawn is able to reach and grab around Rodrigo's neck with his arm, Rodrigo should *never* wrap his arms around Shawn's chest. That will only prevent Rodrigo from having the necessary space to escape.

Should Shawn grab Rodrigo around the neck, Rodrigo applies the following option:

1 Rodrigo places his right elbow on the mat near Shawn's hip so that his right forearm is at 90° with the ground and the right hand is on Shawn's left hip.

2 Pushing off his left foot, Rodrigo escapes his hips to the left and places his left arm in front of Shawn's chest so that his left hand is on Shawn's left shoulder and the forearm is under Shawn's throat. Again, by raising the left elbow Rodrigo will press his forearm against Shawn's Adam's apple and force him to move back, creating space for a guard replacement.

Replacing the guard from the turtle position: Roll over

Being able to effectively replace the guard is a great ability in Jiu-Jitsu. Since one cannot defend the guard forever, chances are that you will, at one time or another, have to roll to your knees and turtle to prevent your guard from being passed. Rodrigo demonstrates here a very simple yet effective way to replace the guard from the turtle position. The roll over uses the same mechanics of the forward roll that you learned from technique #4.

1 Rodrigo is on all fours in the turtle position with Shawn on his right side. Since Shawn's chest is off to the side, his weight is on his knees and not on Rodrigo's back, giving Rodrigo the opening to use the roll over.

2 Since Shawn is on his right side, Rodrigo will roll over his right shoulder. Rodrigo tucks his right arm in and plants the left hand on the mat next to his head while extending the left leg back with the toes pushing off the mat. Rodrigo pushes off the left hand and left foot and rolls over his right shoulder. Shawn needs to let go of his left arm wrap around Rodrigo's waist otherwise he will be forced to roll over as well or have his arm be torqued around the left shoulder in a kimura-type motion. Rodrigo uses the right leg pressing against Shawn's left side to help swing his body around in a clockwise motion around Shawn. His left leg swings out in a semi-circle, creating additional momentum for his roll.

3 At the end of Rodrigo's roll his left leg swings all the way around until it reaches Shawn's right side. Since Rodrigo's right leg was used as one of the pivot points it was perfectly positioned to allow Rodrigo to close his legs around Shawn's waist and replace the guard.

SWEEPS & REVERSALS

While the Gracie Jiu-Jitsu practitioner is comfortable fighting from the bottom with the guard position they undoubtedly prefer to fight from the top. The guard is an effective position to fight when on the bottom but reversing the position and being on top is much better. Additionally, one cannot expect to be able to defend the guard and be successful at fending off a competent attacker forever, so effective means to reverse the position or, better yet, submit the opponent are a must in any fighter's arsenal. A good guard is comprised of good defense, good replacement, sweeps and submission. Generally speaking, the sweeps and submissions from the guard set each other up. When the opponent counters one sweep or a series of sweeps, he leaves himself open for a submission and vice-versa.

Sweeps works best when they are properly set up. Make sure you either force your opponent to lean the way of your sweep with a set up move or watch his weight and body position to apply the correct sweep.

In order to sweep your opponent, most of the time you need to block your opponent's ability to brace to one side in order to sweep him to that side. Always look to trap or block your opponent's arm and leg or knee to one side when attempting a sweep.

Scissor sweep

The scissor sweep is one of the most basic and solid sweeps from the guard. The scissor is one of the first sweeps you will learn and it usually becomes a staple for the white and blue belt. Then it is somewhat forgotten as you progress in belts, as it is viewed as too simplistic and easy to defend. That is far from the truth: the scissor, if properly set up in combination with a choke or when used at the right time, is a very effective sweep that will not only yield a reversal but also end up with you in the mounted position.

1 Rodrigo has Shawn in his closed guard. His right hand holds Shawn's right lapel and the left hand holds Shawn's left sleeve at the elbow. The right hand holding the lapel is very important because the threat of the choke will keep Shawn's focus on defending it. Shawn's right arm is occupied with pressing against Rodrigo's left biceps to block Rodrigo's left hand from attacking the neck for the choke.

2 Rodrigo opens his legs and uses the pressure of his thighs against Shawn's hips to move his hips to the right. Rodrigo may plant the right foot on the mat to help move his hips even farther right should he deem it necessary. Rodrigo inserts the right knee in front of Shawn's hips, leaving the right foot hooked on the outside of Shawn's left hip to prevent him from moving towards Rodrigo's right and passing the guard. Rodrigo's left leg bent at the knee drops to the mat with his calf touching Shawn's right knee. Notice that Rodrigo's hips are away from Shawn's hips; this is another very important detail as the distance allows Rodrigo's right leg to be somewhat extended so his kicking motion has greater power. If Rodrigo's his hips were closer to Shawn, his right leg would be curled in with the foot touching his buttocks and he would have very little power with the same forward kicking motion.

3 Rodrigo pulls Shawn forward, putting Shawn's weight on Rodrigo's right shin while scissoring the legs, kicking the right forward and the left back. The left leg strikes Shawn's right knee, taking away any bracing effect, causing Shawn to be swept to his right with Rodrigo ending up on top in the mounted position.

Reverse angle:

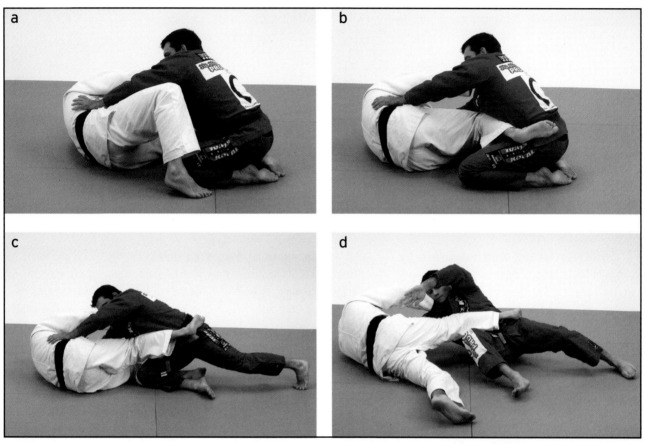

Notice Rodrigo's leg movement: the right foot plants out and helps the hips move further to the right, allowing him to turn his body to the left. Also notice the distance between Rodrigo's hips and Shawn's hips allowing Rodrigo to have the right leg semi-extended so he has more power with the kicking motion. Also notice the scissoring motion of Rodrigo's legs. This uses the same movement as technique #3. Rodrigo plants his left toes on the mat and pushes off them to get on top.

Incorrect: Notice that Rodrigo's hips are too close to Shawn's and his heel is close to his buttocks. He doesn't have adequate power when he tries to kick forward.

62

Butterfly guard hook sweep

The hook sweep is the main sweep from the butterfly or sitting guard. The hook sweep uses many of the same principles previously discussed, such as distance between the hips, escaping the hip to the side, and scissoring the legs to help turn the body. Many of those movements are fundamentals that are involved throughout the techniques of Gracie Jiu-Jitsu. By recognizing such power moves you should eventually be able to correct and improve any difficulties you may find in your techniques. Other keys to the hook sweep are blocking the opponent's side opposite to the hook and sweeping at 45° and to the side.

1 Rodrigo has Shawn in his butterfly or sitting guard with his head in front of Shawn's chest. Rodrigo wants to sweep Shawn to the left so he slides his hips to the right, hooks the right foot under Shawn's left thigh and grabs Shawn's belt with the right hand. At the same time Rodrigo blocks Shawn's right arm from bracing by holding it with his left arm. Notice the position of Rodrigo's left foot: the leg is bent with the foot back near the buttocks and not extended forward.

2 Rodrigo drops his head and left shoulder to the mat as he kicks up with his right leg, lifting Shawn's left leg with it and forcing him to fall to his own right. At the same time Rodrigo pushes and tucks Shawn's right arm to keep him from using it to brace and stop the sweep. As Shawn starts to lose his balance he may fight to regain it, so Rodrigo kicks the left leg back, plants the toes on the mat and pushes off them to continue turning the body. He uses his right foot to help force Shawn's body forward. Rodrigo continues the rotation until he ends up on top of Shawn in the mounted position.

a

b

c

d

2 Correct starting position: Notice how Rodrigo has his hips back and the head forward and low. Rodrigo's head should be in front of Shawn's chest for best results.

2 Reverse angle: Notice the movement from the reverse angle. Rodrigo drives Shawn's right wrist between his legs forcing him off-balance. Also notice how Rodrigo drops his head and left shoulder to initiate the sweep to the side and not straight back.

2 Incorrect starting position: Rodrigo's back is straight so his hips and head are in a perpendicular line. Rodrigo's head may end up above Shawn's shoulder and not in the best position to block Shawn from putting his weight forward and flattening Rodrigo.

2 Incorrect: A very common mistake that occurs when executing the hook sweep is to pull the opponent over you as you try to sweep him. This puts your back flat on the ground and brings the opponent's entire body weight on top of your legs, smothering them. The correct sweeping motion is to the side. As you move your hips to one side, your opponent's weight is already falling forward in the space that you vacated, so sweep at 45° angle and over the shoulder.

Butterfly guard hook sweep: Opponent counters opening the leg

Many times when attempting a hook sweep your opponent will
quickly counter by opening the leg out and planting the foot to stop
the sweep. In that case you should quickly change and apply this
"throw out the trash" sweep.

1 Rodrigo attempts to sweep Shawn to the left with a right hook sweep but Shawn reacts quickly, opening his right leg out
and planting the right foot wide on the mat, blocking the sweep.

2 Without releasing his right foot hook pressure on Shawn's left leg, Rodrigo swings his torso to his left and reaches with
his left arm under Shawn's right leg until he can hook the leg at the knee. Pushing off his left heel, Rodrigo slides his body
under Shawn's body. Rodrigo steps to his left with the left leg and pushes off the foot as he drives Shawn's body up over the
top of his own body. He does this by kicking up with the right hook on Shawn's left leg and reaching up with his left arm under
Shawn's right leg, looping the leg over his head. At this point Rodrigo has propelled Shawn over the top of his body and Shawn
is now on the verge of falling to the other side.

3 Rodrigo continues to push off his left foot and lift Shawn's right leg with the left arm. At the same time he pulls the left side in with his right hand while turning Shawn over to his back, completing the sweep.

Reverse:
Notice Rodrigo's leg and arms movement. He pushes off the left foot and kicks up with the right leg while pulling Shawn's shoulder with his right hand and lifting Shawn's right leg with the left arm to move Shawn over the top of his body and reverse him on to his back.

Overhead sweep

Often times when you attempt a sweep against a standing opponent, your opponent will come forward and throw his weight back
towards you to avoid being swept. Any time that occurs and you can
see your opponent's head directly above your chest, it is time to
use the overhead sweep. In this case Rodrigo attempts the double

ankle grab sweep grabbing Shawn's ankles with both hands while
using the legs to push Shawn's hips back. Since Shawn cannot step
back he would fall backwards, however in this case Shawn counters
by moving his weight forward.

1 Rodrigo attempts to use the double ankle grab sweep on Shawn: his hands hold the back of Shawn's ankles while his feet push
Shawn's hips back. Shawn counters by leaning forward using his weight against Rodrigo's legs and using both hands to grab
Rodrigo's collar to maintain his balance and position. At this point Rodrigo not only feels Shawn's weight coming forward but he also
sees Shawn's head getting close to the imaginary line straight up from his chest. Rodrigo quickly curls his legs in and back slightly.
Since Shawn's weight was already coming forward Shawn leans over Rodrigo's body even more. At this point Shawn's eyes are right
above Rodrigo's eyes and he is ready to fly!

Rodrigo changes his hand grip from Shawn's ankles to the back of the sleeves and pulls them down, forcing Shawn's torso in the same direction. In one quick burst Rodrigo extends his legs, pushing Shawn's hips up and over his head, while pulling Shawn's sleeves up and out, opening Shawn's elbows. This motion sends Shawn flying over Rodrigo's head, Rodrigo follows Shawn's body and rolls over his right shoulder, using the same motion as the backward roll (tech # 4) and ends up landing mounted on Shawn. Notice that Rodrigo rolls over the shoulder and not over the head and also that throughout the rolling motion Rodrigo stays connected to Shawn, maintaining contact with his feet and hands on Shawn's hips and arms until he lands in the mounted position.

Windmill sweep

Another great basic sweep from the guard is the windmill sweep. In the windmill sweep, like in most sweeps, setting up the technique is the key. Once you have set up the move you can take advantage of the slightest motion from the opponent to initiate the sweep and reverse the position. In this case Rodrigo is ready for Shawn's move and does not use the normal set up. Instead, he quickly reacts to

Shawn's initial move to stand up to execute the sweep. One of the most important keys to the windmill sweep is to make sure your sweeping motion is towards your outside shoulder at a 45° angle. Otherwise, if you sweep to the side, your opponent will be able to open his leg, brace and stop the sweep.

1 Rodrigo has Shawn in his closed guard with his right hand gripping Shawn's right collar and the left hand controlling the sleeve right above the elbow. Since he is controlling Shawn's right sleeve Rodrigo will sweep to his left (Shawn's right). Rodrigo waits for Shawn to move.

2 Shawn steps out with his left leg as he attempts to stand and pass Rodrigo's guard. Rodrigo quickly slides his right arm under Shawn's left leg.

3 The following steps are one continuous motion. Rodrigo first opens his legs, swinging the left leg out and raising the right leg up to Shawn's left armpit as he pulls Shawn's torso to his right by the right arm. Using the momentum of the left leg swing to initiate the sweep, Rodrigo kicks his right leg down and across at a 45° angle towards where his left shoulder originally was. At the same time Rodrigo lifts Shawn's left leg with his right arm and pulls his right arm in with the left hand, pulling Shawn off-balance and forcing him to fall to his right. As Shawn falls to his right, Rodrigo continues with the windmill motion – his right leg swinging towards the direction of the sweep while the left swings back under Shawn's body. He uses his right hand to push Shawn's left leg over. Rodrigo completes the sweep, ending up mounted on Shawn.

Reverse angle: Notice how Rodrigo uses his right arm to wrap under Shawn's left leg to pull his head towards that leg so his body is at 90° with Shawn's body, giving him the proper angle for the sweep. The same arm then lifts the leg over in a circular motion for the sweep. Also note Rodrigo's leg motion: the left leg swinging out and then back while the right leg chops down on Shawn's right side.

Windmill sweep to arm-lock

Many times when executing the windmill sweep the opponent resists the sweeping motion by trying to brace his outside leg and extending his arm to maintain his balance. That is the perfect time to go for the arm-lock.

1 As Rodrigo starts the windmill sweep Shawn fights the sweep and extends his right arm to push off and maintain his balance.

2 Rodrigo quickly reacts to Shawn's attempt to regain balance and attacks his extended arm by looping the left leg over Shawn's head, locking in the arm-lock. Rodrigo can either apply the arm-lock immediately or, as he does here, continue with the sweep by driving the left leg down against Shawn's head. This forces Shawn to yield the reversal. Rodrigo can then apply the arm-lock once Shawn's back is on the mat by extending his torso back and driving his hips up against Shawn's right elbow for the lock. Notice that Rodrigo leans to his right and maintains control over Shawn's leg with his left hand to prevent Shawn from using his leg to attempt an escape.

Windmill sweep variation

In this case Rodrigo sets up the sweep by holding Shawn's gi at the left ankle. He waits for Shawn's slightest shift in weight toward standing, which is Rodrigo's cue to initiate the sweep. The advantage of this method is that you do not have to wait for the opponent to raise his leg to initiate the sweep, making it easier to execute it at the proper time. The disadvantage is that many times the wise opponent will fight and attempt to break the grip on the leg to foil the sweep. If your opponent allows you to control that grip, then he is going to be swept.

1 Rodrigo has Shawn in his closed guard. With his right hand he grabs Shawn's gi pants near the left ankle while his left hand grabs Shawn's right sleeve above the elbow. Since Shawn allowed Rodrigo the set up, Rodrigo just waits for Shawn to shift his weight.

a

2 As soon as Shawn shifts his weight either to stand up or to adjust his base, Rodrigo initiates the sweep. He pulls Shawn's left leg out in a circular motion as he opens his legs, then swings the left leg out to create momentum and raises his right leg up towards Shawn's left shoulder. Rodrigo chops across and over with the right leg driving against Shawn's left ribcage as he continues to use his right hand to pull Shawn's left leg over, forcing the reversal. At the end of the motion Rodrigo ends up mounted on Shawn.

b

c

Windmill sweep from the open guard

The same windmill sweep can be applied from a variety of guard stances, both closed and open. In this case Rodrigo uses a slightly modified butterfly guard with his left shin pressing against Shawn's right arm, but the same move works from several different open guard stances. The same principles as the previous version of the windmill guard apply: the first is to set up the sweep by reaching the grips, and second is to initiate the sweeping motion once the opponent shifts his weight.

1 Rodrigo has Shawn in his guard. He is using a modified butterfly guard with his left shin pressing against Shawn's right biceps and the right foot hooked under Shawn's left hip. Rodrigo seeks and is able to grab Shawn's gi pants near the left ankle while his left hand controls Shawn's right arm by gripping the wrist.

2 In reaction to Shawn's weight change Rodrigo opens his left leg out, forcing the shin against Shawn's right arm, and pulls the right wrist in with his left hand. At the same time Rodrigo pulls Shawn's left leg open in a circular motion driving it over in a clockwise direction as he kicks his right foot up. This drives Shawn's hips over, causing the reversal.

Windmill sweep from the butterfly guard: Opponent reacts

Many times when you attempt the windmill sweep from the butterfly guard or even when maintaining the guard, the smart opponent will try crushing both legs together in his attempt to pass your guard. When that occurs, take advantage and immediately use this option.

1 Rodrigo has Shawn in his open guard, using the same variation as in the previous technique. His right foot is hooked under Shawn's left hip, his left shin is pressed against Shawn's right biceps. Rodrigo's right hand grabs Shawn's pants near the left ankle and his right hand controls the right sleeve at the wrist.

2 As Rodrigo attempts to use the windmill sweep on Shawn, reversing him to the left, Shawn opens his right leg out, planting the foot wide and blocking the sweep. Having blocked the sweep, Shawn starts applying pressure with his right shoulder on Rodrigo's left leg trying to collapse it against the right one to pass his guard. Rodrigo maintains his right hand grip on Shawn's gi pants at all times.

3 Rodrigo switches his right foot hook from under Shawn's hip to his ribcage and pushes off it to spin his body to his right. Then in a sudden move, Rodrigo kicks the left leg out from pressing against Shawn's arm as he drives his left arm towards his head. At the same time he drags Shawn's right arm across his body. Rodrigo ends up on Shawn's right side. Rodrigo extends the right leg, plants the toes of both feet on the mat and uses them to push himself on top of Shawn while his right hand pulls Shawn's left leg across his body. Rodrigo finishes the sweep by pulling Shawn's right arm across his body while continuing to pull the left leg in, forcing him to his back.

3 Reverse angle: Notice Rodrigo's leg movement as he uses his right foot hook to spin his body to his right and then kicks out the left leg. This releases the pressure against Shawn's right arm and allows Rodrigo to pull it up and over his head with the left hand. Then notice Rodrigo's leg switch with the left leg going over the top while the right scissors under as he turns to his stomach.

Spider guard scissors sweep

A great use of the scissors sweep can be found in the spider guard.
Rodrigo applies the spider guard pressure on Shawn's arms, taking
him off-balance, and then scissoring the leg to force him to fall.

1 Rodrigo has Shawn in his closed guard. His hands hold Shawn's sleeves at the wrist. He opens the legs, plants the right foot on
the mat and pushes off it, escaping his hips to the right to create space for his legs to come in and go to the spider guard.

2 Rodrigo coils his left leg and places the foot on Shawn's right hip. He then coils the right leg and slides the foot under Shawn's
left arm placing it against the biceps, completing the spider guard stance. Rodrigo pushes off his legs while pulling the arms,
applying pressure on Shawn and forcing his body to lean forward off-balance.

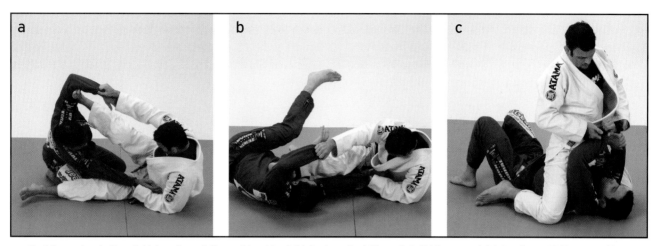

3 Rodrigo extends the right leg, forcefully pushing his right foot against Shawn's left biceps and driving it up. At the same time Rodrigo releases the left foot pressing against Shawn's right hip and drops the leg to the mat while pulling Shawn's right arm across with his left hand, thus forcing Shawn's body to twist counterclockwise. As Shawn struggles to regain his balance Rodrigo applies the final touch – kicking the left leg in a scissoring motion against Shawn's right leg, chopping it off the mat and forcing him to fall to the left. Rodrigo completes the movement still pulling up on Shawn's sleeves using the momentum of the fall to follow Shawn's motion and end up mounted on top.

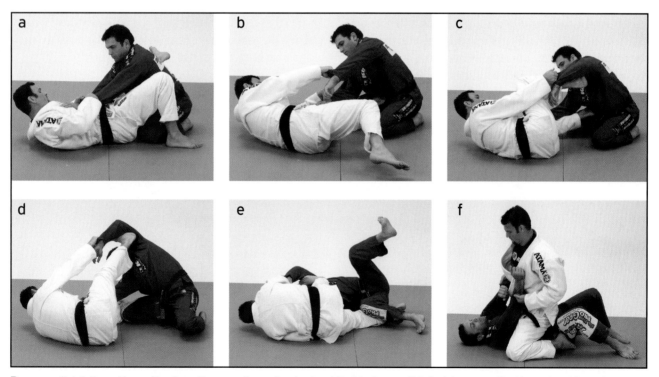

Reverse: Watch the entire motion from the opposite angle: check out Rodrigo's use of his feet to escape the hips out and then place them on Shawn's right hip and left biceps. Notice Rodrigo's upwards kicking extension of the right leg. It drives Shawn's left arm up, causing the shoulder to turn, as he drops the left leg and scissors it across the knee, removing Shawn's last balance point.

Open guard tripod sweep

The tripod sweep is a staple of the open guard. Rodrigo uses Shawn's reaction to the pressure of the feet against the top part of his body. While pulling the arm, Rodrigo trips Shawn by placing a block behind Shawn's foot and pushing the body with the other foot.

Notice again that in order to sweep, Rodrigo must block one side of Shawn's body and sweep to that direction. In this case Rodrigo takes away Shawn's ability to walk back by blocking the back of both feet.

1 Rodrigo has Shawn in his open guard. His right foot pushes against the left biceps, the left foot pushes against Shawn's right hip, the right hand is pulling on Shawn's right collar and the left hand is pulling on Shawn's right sleeves. Note that the difference between the open and the spider guard in the previous technique is subtle, it is based on controlling one arm and the collar (open) or controlling both arms with the foot pressing against at least one biceps (spider).

2 Shawn reacts to the pressure by trying to raise his torso. Sensing his reaction, Rodrigo decides to go for the tripod sweep. He pushes off his feet to turn his body to the left. Rodrigo then releases his left hand grip on Shawn's right sleeve, grabbing the back of the right ankle instead. This prevents Shawn from being able to step back with the right foot.

3 Having effectively blocked Shawn's right foot, Rodrigo turns his attention to blocking the left foot. He drops his right leg down to the mat and hooks his foot behind Shawn's left foot. Now Shawn cannot step back, Rodrigo then pushes forward with his left leg, driving the foot against Shawn's hip and thereby driving Shawn's body back. Rodrigo pulls in his right foot, lifting Shawn's left foot from the mat and causing him to fall backwards.

4 Rodrigo continues with the push-pull motion and follows Shawn's body as he falls, using his momentum to pull himself up and over Shawn. Notice that Rodrigo falls to his own left side so he remains close to Shawn as he starts to pull himself over to the mount. Should Rodrigo try to move straight over he would have to go to his knees, allowing a lot of space for Shawn to pull his leg in to replace the guard or to block Rodrigo from mounting.

5 Rodrigo continues to move forward and to his left as slides his left leg over Shawn's right leg. He keeps his right foot on the mat with the knee pointing up so his right shin blocks Shawn's left leg. This prevents Shawn from closing his leg around Rodrigo's right leg and achieving half-guard. Rodrigo drives Shawn's right wrist across his body, pinning it to the far right and forcing Shawn to turn his body in that direction. This makes it easy for Rodrigo to loop the right leg over Shawn's left leg and achieve the mount. Pay special attention to Rodrigo's move of pinning Shawn's arm across his body to force the body to one direction. This is similar to what he points out on his guard concept #2 where he pushes the leg across instead. Make a mental note and use these concepts when trying to control your opponent at the end of a sweep, when he is trying to escape from the bottom or in passing the guard.

Reverse angle: Notice how Rodrigo turns his body to his right so the angle of his push with the left leg and block with the right foot are their most effective as he kicks Shawn's right foot forward while pushing the hips back. Also notice how Rodrigo follows Shawn's fall and drops to his right to keep his body close to Shawn and prevent him from coiling the legs to block the move to the mount.

Tripod sweep to sickle sweep

Many times when attempting the tripod sweep your opponent will counter it by pushing his front hip forward, deflecting the push from your foot against his hips. When that occurs change to the sickle sweep.

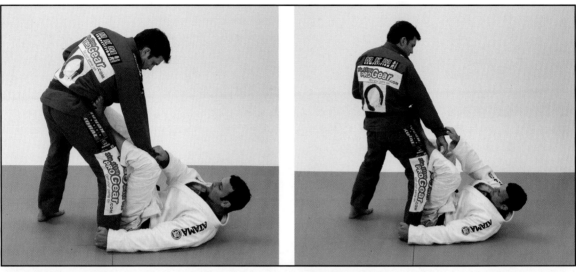

1 Rodrigo has Shawn in his open guard. He sets up the tripod sweep by grabbing the back of Shawn's right heel with his left hand, and uses his right hand to control Shawn's right sleeve while his left foot pushes against Shawn's right hip. Sensing the tripod sweep coming, Shawn counters it by driving his hips forward and straightening his body.

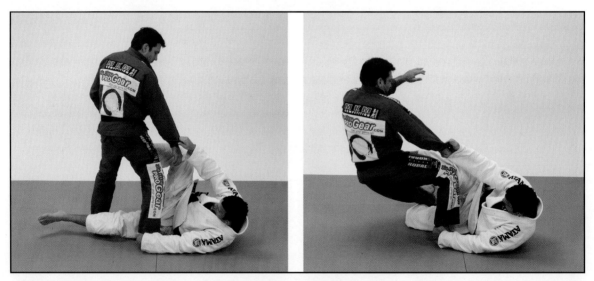

2 Rodrigo quickly reacts to Shawn's counter by switching to the sickle sweep. He places his right foot on Shawn's left thigh while at the same time he drops his left leg down to the mat between Shawn's legs. In one motion Rodrigo kicks the left leg back, using it like a sickle hitting the back of Shawn's left heel and removing that base. At the same time Rodrigo pushes with the right foot against Shawn's thigh forcing him to fall backwards.

3 Rodrigo uses Shawn's falling momentum to help pull himself up, ending up on top with the completed sweep and ready to pass Shawn's guard.

Reverse view:

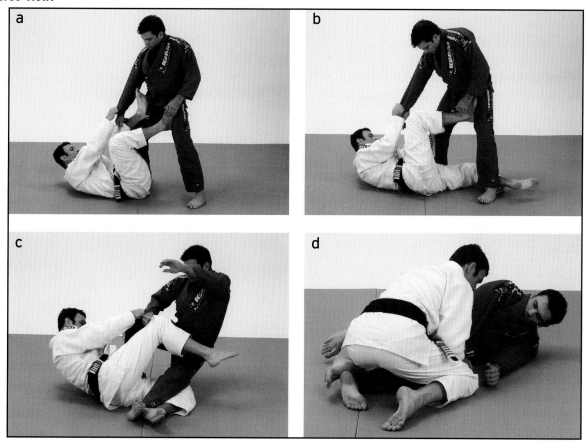

Notice how Rodrigo causes Shawn to fall by kicking back and hitting Shawn's left heel as he pushes forward with his right foot against Shawn's left thigh. Also notice how Rodrigo uses Shawn's falling momentum to pull himself up by maintaining the grip on Shawn's right sleeve with his right hand.

73

Handstand sweep

The handstand sweep is one of the best sweeps for when your opponent stands up. In the handstand sweep you push off your hand to apply your weight to the opponent's near leg while blocking his foot from being able to step back. The best time to use the handstand sweep is as soon as your opponent stands up but before he has time to get completely set in base.

1 Rodrigo has Shawn in his closed guard. In his attempt to break open and pass Rodrigo's guard, Shawn stands up. Rodrigo immediately attacks Shawn's base with the handstand sweep. He turns his torso to his left, lassoes his left arm around Shawn's right leg and grabs his own left lapel with that hand to fully take away Shawn's ability to move that leg.

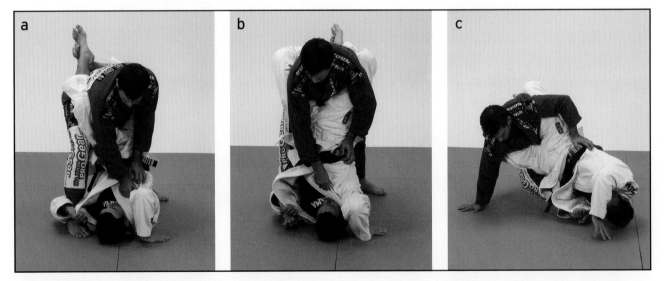

2 Rodrigo plants his left hand above his head and pushes off it, twisting his body and driving his hips and the weight of his body against Shawn's right leg, forcing Shawn to fall back. In this case Shawn is quick to react and uses his right hand to break his fall.

3 Rodrigo reaches with his right hand and grabs Shawn's right sleeve at the wrist. He pulls Shawn's right arm from the mat, forcing Shawn to drop his back to the mat and complete the fall. Notice that Rodrigo continues to turn his body to the left and raises his torso to the right to keep Shawn's right leg off the mat, preventing him from trying to get back up.

4 Once Rodrigo's hips turn over the top he has effectively won the battle for position. He can release his left arm from around Shawn's right leg and use the left hand planted back on the mat to help prop his body up until he ends up mounted on Shawn. Notice that Rodrigo never releases his right hand grip on Shawn's right wrist sleeve, using it to help bring his body over the top and also to turn and control Shawn's torso. This prevents Shawn from turning to his left in his attempt to get back up.

Omoplata sweep

At times when applying the handstand sweep, the smart opponent will quickly counter by bending the leg and driving his knee in. In that case you should switch to the omoplata sweep. The omoplata sweep can be used alone as well as in combination with the handstand and the star sweep.

1 As Shawn stands up Rodrigo tries to set up the handstand sweep, lassoing his left arm around Shawn's right leg. Shawn counters Rodrigo's move by bending the right leg and angling his knee in towards Rodrigo's hips, making it difficult for Rodrigo to drop his weight on that leg. Rodrigo quickly opts for the omoplata sweep as he passes Shawn's right arm to his left hand. Now with his right arm and hand Rodrigo controls Shawn's right side.

a

2 Rodrigo opens his legs and swings the right leg around, using it to move his body in a clockwise direction. Notice that as he spins to his left Rodrigo's left leg hooks under Shawn's right armpit to set up the omoplata sweep. Once his body is nearly parallel to Shawn's, Rodrigo kicks down with his left leg, driving it against Shawn's right arm and forcing him to roll forward over the shoulder. Rodrigo follows the motion as he sits up, ending up sitting next to Shawn. He is still controlling the right leg and arm with his left arm.

b

c

3 Rodrigo pulls his right leg back, plants the foot on the ground and pushes off it to drive his body over Shawn. Rodrigo switches arms, his right arm now around Shawn's right leg, and pulls his left leg back under his hips as he turns his body so it faces Shawn. Rodrigo ends up in side control.

Summersault sweep

The summersault sweep is a very dynamic and spectacular sweep. It can be used alone or as a counter to the opponent's reaction of raising his body while driving the hips forward to counter the omo-plata sweep. When properly executed, the summersault sweep yields a reversal and good positioning.

1 As Rodrigo attempts the omoplata sweep, Shawn counters it by driving his hips forward while raising his torso up, effectively taking away the power of Rodrigo's left leg against his right arm.

2 Shawn's reaction puts his weight back. Sensing this, Rodrigo opts to switch to the summersault sweep. He plants his right hand on the mat next to his right ear and kicks the right leg back to help summersault back over his left shoulder. Rodrigo ends up kneeling next to Shawn with his legs on each side of Shawn's right leg. The left arm wrapped around Shawn's right leg is still grabbing Shawn's right sleeve. Rodrigo raises his torso pulling Shawn's right foot off the ground, forcing him to fall backwards. Notice that Shawn has been in a precarious position from the start: Rodrigo controls Shawn's right wrist up to the point when he extends his body and Shawn falls back.

3 Rodrigo switches hands: his left hand now grabs Shawn's collar to control the upper body and his right hand grabs Shawn's right leg pants at the calf, lifting it to keep Shawn's back on the mat and preventing him from getting up. Rodrigo turns his body so it faces down and brings his knees in next to Shawn's body, reaching side control.

76

Leg trap sweep

It is never a good idea to allow your opponent to stand up but at times you can't stop him. It is important, therefore, to have some techniques to break his balance *before* he gets his base set and is ready to pass your guard. You want to take advantage of the moment just as the opponent stands up or when he closes his legs trying to place a knee inside your legs to break the guard open. A great technique that works at such times is the leg trap sweep. The key to this sweep is to make sure you trap the legs at the knees and not below them. Otherwise the opponent can easily break the trap and even go directly to the mounted position.

1 Rodrigo has Shawn in his closed guard and controls both wrists with his hands. Shawn manages to stand up. Shawn brings his legs together as he tries to place one knee forward between Rodrigo's legs to break open Rodrigo's legs. Now is the time to go for the leg trap sweep.

2 While still maintaining wrist control, Rodrigo quickly opens his legs and drops them, re-closing them around Shawn's knees. Rodrigo then crosses Shawn's arms in front of him. At this point Shawn has no way to brace a fall to either side so Rodrigo can choose on which side he wants to drop Shawn.

3 Rodrigo pushes Shawn's arms up and to the left, forcing him to fall to that side. Once Shawn hits the mat Rodrigo releases his right hand and uses it to grab Shawn's back so he can't escape his body away. Rodrigo gets himself up and over Shawn by using his left hand to pull Shawn's right arm across while extending his legs.

Notice how important it is to bind the legs at the knees:

Correct: Rodrigo traps Shawn's legs right at the knees.

Incorrect: Rodrigo traps the legs below the knees. Shawn simply opens his knees out and drops them over Rodrigo's thighs, reaching the mounted position.

Leg spread sweep

A very effective variation of the placement of your legs when using the open guard is to grapevine one of your legs around the opponent's front leg. This is sometimes referred to as the De La Riva guard. The outside/inside hook allows you to control the distance between you and your opponent by being able to pull him in by the hook or push him away by extending the leg. This is an advanced use of the legs and while many sweeps can generate from this position it also exposes your grapevined leg to knee bars and foot locks, so be careful when using this placement.

The leg spread sweep takes advantage of the control that this type of guard gives you, by allowing you to push away your opponent's far leg while keeping the front leg close, thereby taking away his base.

1 Side view of the hook placement: Rodrigo's left leg grapevines around Shawn's right leg with the foot hooked under the thigh. His right foot pushes against Shawn's left hip.

1 Rodrigo drops his right foot to the inside of Shawn's left thigh while his right hand grabs the back of the right collar and his left hand controls Shawn's right arm, gripping the sleeve just above the elbow. Rodrigo initiates the leg spread by pushing Shawn's left leg away with his right foot while at the same time pulling his collar down and forward, breaking his balance.

2 Rodrigo continues to extend his right leg, pushing Shawn's left leg away and pulling Shawn's collar forward with the right hand. Rodrigo kicks his left leg forward using his left leg and the foot hooked around Shawn's right leg to drive him further forward and forcing him to fall over his left shoulder.

3 As Shawn's body hits the mat, Rodrigo wraps his left arm around Shawn's back. He releases the left foot hook from Shawn's right thigh, looping the leg over Shawn to reach the mounted position.

Reverse angle:

Notice how Rodrigo extends his right leg and pushes Shawn's right leg away while still maintaining the left foot hook around Shawn's right leg. Only when Shawn hits the mat does Rodrigo release the hook and push off the foot to loop it over for the mount.

HALF-GUARD SWEEPS

The half-guard is a transitory position between passing the guard or having the guard replaced. If you have top position, you want to either pass the half-guard or submit your opponent. If you are on the bottom you want to replace the guard, or sweep or submit your opponent. The half-guard top is when you have one leg trapped between the opponent's legs, while in the half-guard bottom your legs are trapping one of your opponent's legs.

Being in the half-guard is a common occurrence in a match. The scrambles and adjustments between the two fighters means often times one ends up with one leg caught. It is important, then, to have a small arsenal of submissions when you are either on top or bottom, sweeps for when you are on the bottom and half-guard passes when you are on top.

Most of the submissions with minor adjustments work from the half-guard whether you are on top or the bottom, so we are not going to repeat them here. You should simply be aware that they are available most of the time.

While many fighters have developed a large arsenal of positions from the half-guard, Rodrigo believes that being on the bottom in the half-guard is a slight disadvantage. Therefore he looks for sweeps to reverse his position from bottom to top or a quick submission. As we have pointed out before, preventing the opponent from reaching around your head with his arm is one of the most important things to do when defending the

guard. This rule remains true when you are defending the half-guard. Taking away that kind of control from your opponent is crucial to using the sweeps and guard replacements.

A key to successfully sweeping someone from the half-guard is to get under them. Since in the half-guard you are trapping one of their legs with both of your legs, you lose your ability to move your hips out in relation to your opponent. To compensate for that you need to get under his body so that he teeters over you, allowing you to control where his weight is and to sweep him to either side. Anytime your opponent is able to move his body away to one side he reaches a more stable position because his weight is resting on the mat. Getting under your opponent both prevents him from becoming stable and sets up the sweep.

Series of sweeps are often tied together in response to the opponent's weight distribution and reaction to an initial move. The half-guard sweeps are even more likely to be connected because of your position under the opponent and your inability to use your feet on the ground to move your hips either out or in. To be effective at sweeping someone in the half-guard, many times you have to switch back and forth between two sweeps until you get ahead of your opponent's reaction and succeed in reversing him.

Here are some of Rodrigo's favorite half-guard sweeps.

78

Half-guard sweep: Foot grab

In this case, Rodrigo defends the half-guard and tries to slip to Shawn's back. If Shawn counters the move then Rodrigo switches to the foot grab sweep.

1 Rodrigo has Shawn's right leg trapped in the half-guard. His left arm is under Shawn's right arm, allowing him to slip to Shawn's back. Should Shawn fail to react, Rodrigo will easily end up on Shawn's back. He can simply drop his body down while driving the left arm up against Shawn's armpit, forcing Shawn's body up, and loop the left leg around Shawn's back, hooking the foot in front of Shawn's left thigh.

2 Instead, Shawn counters the move by wrapping his right arm around Rodrigo's left arm, blocking his downward path. Rodrigo uses his right arm as a frame to prevent Shawn from moving his left knee up and closing the gap.

3 Realizing his path to the back is blocked, Rodrigo drops his left arm down, wrapping it around Shawn's right thigh. He then slips his right hand under Shawn's left shin grabbing the ankle and pulling the leg in until he can grab Shawn's right foot with his left hand. Notice that at this point Rodrigo traps Shawn's right leg with his legs, and the left leg with his hands. Rodrigo slides the noose of his legs around Shawn's right leg to below the knee and stretches his legs, pulling Shawn's right leg back to the left with them.

4 Rodrigo then releases the figure 4 noose as he loops the left leg over Shawn's right leg and extends his right leg down. Rodrigo changes his right hand from Shawn's left ankle, instead grabbing the outside of the left knee. Rodrigo then pushes off his right foot to help spin his body around Shawn's body while pulling Shawn's left knee in with his right hand and the left foot with his left hand. At the same time, Rodrigo drives his left shoulder against the right side of Shawn's torso, forcing Shawn to fall with his back on the mat.

Reverse angle of the movement:

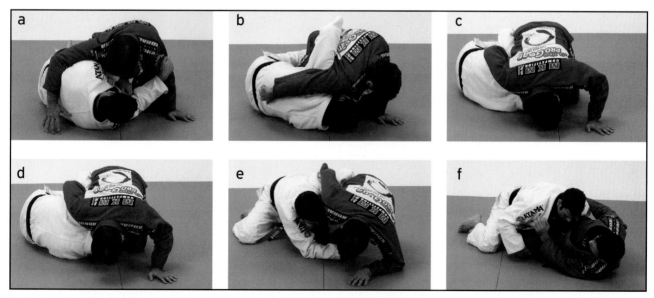

Notice how Rodrigo first tries to slip to Shawn's back by driving his left arm up, and only switches to the sweep when Shawn counters by wrapping his right arm and blocking the path to the back. Also notice how Rodrigo uses the right hand to pull Shawn's left knee in, breaking his base, and forcing him to fall to that side.

Half-grab sweep: Roll-over

At times when faced with the imminent sweep of the foot grab, the opponent will push off with his free hand to avoid being swept back. This drives his weight away from the trapped foot and on top of his opponent. In that case take advantage of your opponent's over-commitment with his weight and use the roll-over sweep.

1 Rodrigo was able to set up the foot grab sweep from the half-guard by reaching around Shawn's right leg and trapping the left foot. Shawn senses he is going to be swept to his left and pushes off his left hand, driving his weight on top of Rodrigo and countering the sweep.

a

b

2 Rodrigo reverses the direction of his roll and rotates to his left, taking Shawn over him for the sweep.

c

3 Rodrigo continues to roll in a counterclockwise direction until he gets on top of Shawn. Notice that Rodrigo still has control over Shawn's left foot with his hands and continues to hold on to it even as he adjusts his right arm around Shawn's hips to control the body. Rodrigo only releases the foot after he traps it with his right leg by driving the knee up so his shin blocks Shawn's left leg. This keeps Shawn from moving and perhaps being able to trap Rodrigo's leg in the half-guard. Notice that it was Shawn's commitment to pushing his weight in the opposite direction of the initial sweep that makes it easy for Rodrigo to roll him over the top. If, as Rodrigo tries the roll over move, Shawn compensates by shifting his weight back to his left, Rodrigo can return to the foot grab sweep direction.

Half-guard sweep: Helicopter

This is one of the most advanced sweeps that we show in this book but it is also one of Rodrigo's favorites sweeps from the half-guard. It is very effective when the opponent manages to get a knee between your legs and is about to break through your half-guard control. From a seemingly bad situation Rodrigo pulls out this helicopter sweep.

1 Rodrigo has Shawn in his half-guard, trapping the right leg between his legs. Shawn got an advantage by moving his knee past the control of Rodrigo's legs and is ready to pass. Should Rodrigo fail to react, Shawn will drive his knee to one side and use his weight and forward body pressure to pass the guard.

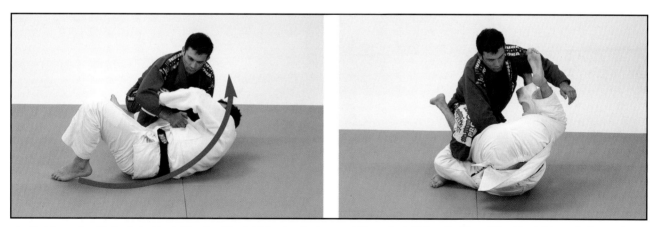

2 Rodrigo spins his body to his right using his right leg to pivot around Shawn's right leg. Rodrigo slides his right arm in front of Shawn's right leg and holds his own gi pants. Rodrigo continues to spin his body until his head is directly in front of Shawn's hips while using the left hand to push under Shawn's left arm. Rodrigo retains control over Shawn's right sleeve with his right hand.

3 Rodrigo uses his left leg as a pendulum, kicking it forward and down. Rodrigo uses the momentum of that swing to help kick his right leg forward, forcing Shawn's body to fall forward as Rodrigo sits up, ending up behind Shawn.

Alternate angle:

Rodrigo coils his left leg under Shawn's legs, leaving his left foot hooked under the hips. He kicks the right leg forward, driving Shawn's right leg in that direction and forcing Shawn to fall further forward. After creating the space with his forward kick and while still holding onto Shawn's right foot, Rodrigo then turns to his right and releases the left foot hook from under Shawn's hips.

4 Rodrigo continues turning to his right until he gets to his knees. Rodrigo starts to stand up while lifting Shawn's right foot to prevent him from being able to stand. Rodrigo completes the sweep standing up while still holding Shawn's right foot. Rodrigo can push the foot to the right and pass Shawn's guard.

Reverse view:

Notice Rodrigo's use of his legs and hands to propel Shawn forward and to get under him. When Rodrigo swings the left leg he uses the swing to help himself up as he kicks the right leg down. Rodrigo's left hand slides behind Shawn's left thigh and helps Rodrigo pull himself under Shawn as Shawn is pushed forward. Also notice that Rodrigo never lets go of the grip on Shawn's right ankle, otherwise Shawn would be able to stand up and walk away and face Rodrigo.

Half-guard sweep: Summersault

A solid variation of the helicopter sweep is the summersault sweep. Rodrigo starts the sweep much in the same manner he does the hel- icopter sweep but instead of sliding under Shawn, Rodrigo rolls over his head.

1 Rodrigo begins the helicopter sweep on Shawn and halfway through the move (step three of the previous technique) he changes to the summersault sweep by rolling over his right shoulder and getting his left leg on the outside of Shawn's left leg.

2 Rodrigo wraps his left arm around Shawn's left leg and continues the roll as he pulls Shawn's legs from under him, ending up with the reversal.

3 Rodrigo sits back and releases his right arm from grabbing around Shawn's right leg, instead placing the elbow next to Shawn's left ribs. Rodrigo then uses his left hand to grab and pin Shawn's right leg to the mat as he loops his left leg over Shawn's legs ending up facing Shawn ready to pass to the left.

Reverse View:

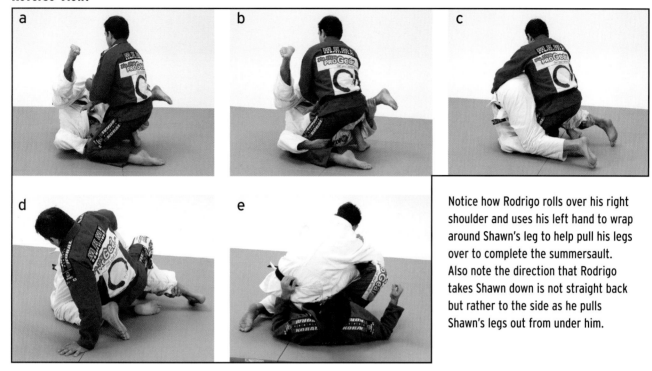

Notice how Rodrigo rolls over his right shoulder and uses his left hand to wrap around Shawn's leg to help pull his legs over to complete the summersault. Also note the direction that Rodrigo takes Shawn down is not straight back but rather to the side as he pulls Shawn's legs out from under him.

Reverse View:

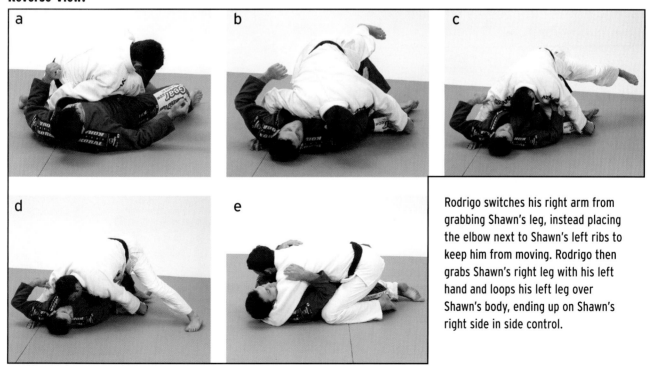

Rodrigo switches his right arm from grabbing Shawn's leg, instead placing the elbow next to Shawn's left ribs to keep him from moving. Rodrigo then grabs Shawn's right leg with his left hand and loops his left leg over Shawn's body, ending up on Shawn's right side in side control.

HALF-GUARD PASSES

All of the elements required for properly defending the half-guard should be avoided when trying to pass it. In other words, never let your opponent get under you. Always try to control his head by reaching and wrapping your arm around the head. Have your weight always to one side of his body. And you may have to switch your body from one side of the opponent to the other as he adjusts his position and gets under you.

One of the keys to passing the half-guard is to pin your opponent's back to the mat and control the hips by controlling one of his legs and then working on breaking his leg grip around your leg.

Again, it is not necessary to have a myriad of specialized half-guard passes. Concentrate your efforts on mastering two or three in order to be successful at dealing with most half-guard passing situations.

Half-guard pass 1: Leg loop

This is a classic half-guard pass. In this guard pass Rodrigo demonstrates all the keys necessary to pass the half-guard. He controls Shawn's upper body with his arm around the head. He pins him flat to the mat with the collar grab under the armpit and works on breaking the leg grip by pushing the outside knee to the opposite direction that he wants to pass.

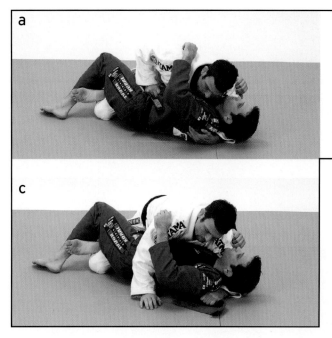

1 Rodrigo is in Shawn's half-guard with his right leg trapped between Shawn's legs. Rodrigo controls Shawn's upper body with his left arm wrapped around the head and the shoulder pushing against the right side of the shin to keep him from turning his head to the right. To further control Shawn's upper body and to keep his back flat on the mat Rodrigo pulls open Shawn's left gi lapel with his right hand and drives it under Shawn's left armpit, passing it to his left hand. With this grip Shawn cannot turn his body to his right as the lapel stops him, nor can he turn to his left as his right arm is trapped under Rodrigo's left arm. Now that Shawn's upper body is completely immobilized Rodrigo will work on breaking open the legs.

2 Rodrigo reaches with his right hand and grabs Shawn's left knee and pushes it down and to Shawn's left, pinning the leg to the mat (again notice the use of pushing the outside leg out to control the hips). Rodrigo turns his hips so they face down, opening the left leg out. Rodrigo uses his left foot to move his body down and to his left in a semicircular motion, forcing his right leg against the back of Shawn's right leg. His right hand pushes Shawn's right knee away, opening the noose around his right leg.

3 Rodrigo then brings the left knee in close to Shawn's right hip. Because of the hip switch Rodrigo's right knee points up instead of down, making it easier for him to push off the right foot and loop the leg away from Shawn's trap. Rodrigo loops the leg back until his foot touches the mat. He then continues to force Shawn's left knee away and brings his knees in and hips square with Shawn's body, completing the pass.

Reverse View:

In this reverse view you can clearly see Rodrigo's use of his legs: the left leg opening out, pushing off the foot to move the body back and down, and forcing his right calf against Shawn's right leg while pushing the left knee in the opposite direction to create the opening to release his leg.

Half-guard pass 2: Hand under

The hand-under pass is as solid a pass as you can have. By controlling the outside leg and keeping the opponent from using it to push off the mat, you effectively kill any possibility of a reaction on his part. This pass is best when executed slowly and deliberately, maintaining full control and balance at all times. The opponent will feel helpless as you progress to the pass, adding a demoralizing effect and breaking his fighting spirit.

1 Rodrigo is in Shawn's half-guard with his right leg trapped between Shawn's legs. Rodrigo's first move is to wrap his left arm around Shawn's head, driving his left shoulder against the right side of the chin to keep Shawn's back flat on the mat.

a

2 Rodrigo then brings his right arm back and wraps it under Shawn's left leg. This is the key to this pass. Rodrigo *has to maintain control* over Shawn's left leg, preventing him from putting the foot on the mat and pushing off it. Rodrigo opens the left leg out and walks his body back and down while pushing Shawn's left leg out with the right arm, using a similar motion as in the previous technique to break open Shawn's legs.

b

c

2 **Reverse view:** Notice Rodrigo's right arm grabbing under Shawn's left leg prevents Shawn from dropping the leg down and using the foot to push off and move his hips.

3 Rodrigo loops his right foot over Shawn's right leg and squares his hips, bringing his knees in close to Shawn's body to complete the pass.

Half-guard pass 3: Hip switch

In this half-guard pass the key is to be able to underhook the opponent's arm. Again, most of the elements and keys to the half-guard passing are present in this pass: you need to keep your weight away from the opponent and pin his hips and body flat to the mat.

1 Rodrigo is in Shawn's half-guard with his right leg trapped. Rodrigo is able to hook his right arm under Shawn's left arm giving him the perfect set-up for the hip switch pass.

2 Rodrigo wants to pin Shawn and prevent him from being able to get his back off the mat and turned to the side. He places his forehead on the ground with his right ear touching Shawn's right ear. Now with his right arm wrapped around Shawn's left arm and his head trapping Shawn's head, Rodrigo has Shawn completely immobilized. Rodrigo opens his left leg out wide of his body, putting his weight to Shawn's right. Rodrigo uses his left arm to pull up on Shawn's right arm to keep his back flat on the mat

3 Rodrigo raises his hips and drives his right knee forward between Shawn's legs. The pressure of Rodrigo's hips driving the leg forward makes it impossible for Shawn to stop Rodrigo's right leg from slipping through. Rodrigo continues to drive his hips forward so they face towards Shawn's head while pulling up on the right arm with his left arm. Since Shawn cannot turn to his right his hips are flat, preventing him from maintaining the pressure on Rodrigo's right leg. Rodrigo's leg slowly slides out from between Shawn's legs. Rodrigo turns his hips down, reaching side control.

Reverse view:

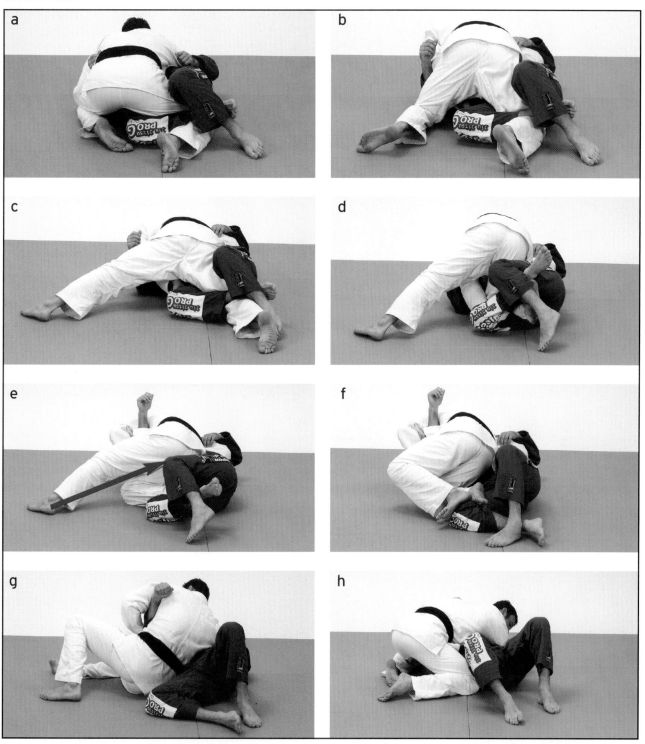

Notice Rodrigo's move to release his leg. He keeps Shawn's back flat on the ground and uses the power of his hips to drive the leg forward until the foot slips out to pass the guard. Should his foot become stuck, Rodrigo can use his left foot to push against Shawn's left knee to give it the last little push and release the foot.

PASSING THE GUARD

Frequently in Gracie Jiu-Jitsu you are either defending the guard or trying to pass it. Since both positions are so important it is imperative to understand what is necessary to be successful in both passing and defending. In this section we will deal with passing the guard. In addition, you can get great insights on what is important for defending the guard as well by simply turning the situation in reverse. By noticing what the passer needs to achieve in order to pass, you can try to neutralize them when you are defending.

The most important thing you can do in order to be successful at passing the guard is to achieve proper posture. Any time your posture is broken, you need to go back and regain it *before* you proceed any further, otherwise you are risking either getting caught in a submission or being swept. Once you have achieved proper posture and everything is in place then you can begin with your passing attempt.

On the knees posture:

Proper Posture

A Rodrigo in proper posture: his shoulders are square, his right arm grips Shawn's collars near the chest and the arm is extended, keeping Shawn from being able to sit up. Rodrigo keeps his right arm relaxed, only applying the pressure when he feels Shawn's attempt to sit up. Rodrigo's left hand grabs Shawn's belt while pressing down on the hip to keep Shawn from moving it. Rodrigo's elbow is down and tight, just inside Shawn's right thigh, and pressing against it. His torso is straight, head erect with the head facing forward.

B Although it appears that Rodrigo's extended right arm is exposed for an arm-lock, it isn't so. Because Rodrigo is in proper posture, when Shawn attempts to go for an arm-lock Rodrigo simply impedes his progress by using his left hand to control the hips, stopping it from going up near the joint and using the left elbow to block Shawn's right leg from coming up to set up the arm-lock.

Improper Posture

A Rodrigo's left hand is grabbing Shawn's chest instead of pinning the hips down. Shawn is able to move his hips to the left and start an arm-lock attack. His left foot pushes against Rodrigo's right hip, raising his hips and bringing his right leg on top of Rodrigo's left shoulder. All Shawn needs to do to complete the arm-lock is to loop his left leg over Rodrigo's head and extend his body.

B Rodrigo's left elbow is open. Shawn can easily break Rodrigo's posture by pulling the elbow forward, causing Rodrigo to fall forward.

C Rodrigo's left elbow is too far inside Shawn's legs and his head is low, causing his back to curve and bringing the torso low. Shawn can easily open his legs and close them back over Rodrigo's left arm for the triangle set-up.

D Rodrigo's left hand does not grip Shawn's belt as he drives the left elbow against the inside of Shawn's right thigh. Once again, without having Rodrigo's left hand pinning his hips, Shawn is able to open and close the legs over Rodrigo's left arm for the triangle.

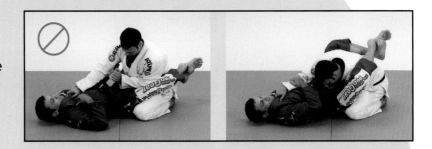

Standing posture:

Correct

Rodrigo steps out with his right leg, planting it next to Shawn's left hip. He then stands up, planting the left foot back and away from Shawn's right hip so that his hips are at an angle in relation to Shawn's. To keep his balance and his base Rodrigo doesn't place his weight on his arms but rather on his legs as he stands up. Rodrigo now has balance and will not fall if Shawn pulls him forward or pushes him back.

Incorrect

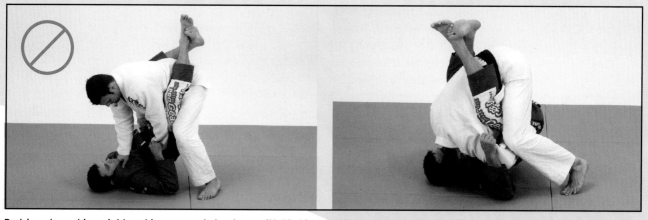

Rodrigo places his weight on his arms and stands up with his hips parallel to Shawn's hips. Notice how Rodrigo is leaning forward, with his weight on his arms, and his feet are at equal distance from Shawn's buttocks. Rodrigo has no base and will easily fall forward when Shawn pulls him.

Another key to passing someone's guard is to be able to control the opponent's hips, keeping him from moving them. You need to change your weight distribution as you progress in the pass and be able to achieve the proper grips in order to control his hips. Proceed one step at a time and only go forward as you reach your goals and feel comfortable. If at any time you sense danger or feel something is out of order, it is better to retreat in order to get your position just right. Proceeding when you sense danger or feel something is not in the proper place will generally result in a submission or a reversal.

Controlling the hip examples:

Correct: Rodrigo's left hand pins Shawn's right leg to the mat while his right hand grabs Shawn's belt, keeping him from moving his hips. Rodrigo reaches Shawn's side in total control while pinning the hips to the mat.

Incorrect: Rodrigo doesn't control Shawn's belt so his hips are free. Even when Rodrigo gets near Shawn's right side, Shawn is able to move his hips out to the left and loop his left leg in front of Rodrigo's head to block the pass and replace the guard.

Correct: Rodrigo has his right arm wrapped around Shawn's left leg with the elbow closed. His left knee pins Shawn's right leg to the mat, effectively taking away Shawn's ability to move his hips.

Incorrect: Rodrigo's right arm is not tight against Shawn's left leg. His elbow is open, allowing Shawn to push the elbow further open, rotate his hips and bring the left leg back in, blocking Rodrigo's pass.

Correct: Rodrigo has his right arm wrapped around Shawn's waist with his torso pressing down on Shawn's legs and hips keeping them pinned.

Incorrect: Rodrigo has his right arm wrapped around Shawn's legs at the knees. Rodrigo controls Shawn's legs instead of the hips, allowing Shawn to maintain his ability to move his hips from one side to the other.

Correct: Rodrigo passes with his left knee through Shawn's legs. Rodrigo slides his left knee on the mat, making sure to maintain his weight on Shawn's hips and keeping his left foot hooked on Shawn's left leg to freeze Shawn's hips.

Incorrect: Rodrigo passes with the left knee through Shawn's legs, but instead of maintaining control of Shawn's hips with his weight on them and the foot hooked on the leg, he has his weight on his left knee and simply pivots the left foot around the knee. This releases the hook and gives Shawn an opening to easily escape his hips and replace the guard.

Keep your opponent's back flat on the mat

Another important thing to do when passing someone's guard is to hold his back flat on the mat as much as possible.

Correct: Rodrigo shows the ideal alignment he wants Shawn's body to have, with his back and hips flat on the mat.

Incorrect: Whenever your opponent is able to turn to his side, he increases his chances of escaping the hips and/or replacing the guard.

Guard pass drill: Toreana or bullfighter's pass

The toreana or bullfighter's pass is one of the most effective and popular passes from the standing position. In it the passer controls the defender's legs with his hands and drives them to one side while stepping around them to the other side to reach side control, like a bullfighter waving his cape in front of the bull. This drill is very important because the key to the toreana is the ability for the passer to quickly execute the deflection and step movement. Otherwise the defender can quickly move his hips, free the legs and replace the guard.

1 Rodrigo stands in front of Shawn, who has his back on the mat. Rodrigo holds both of Shawn's gi pants on the inside right at the knees. The hand position is crucial for the toreana pass to work. Hold too high towards the hips and the opponent can easily circle the lower legs and hook over your arms, stopping your ability to move around the legs. Hold the legs too low and close to the ankles and the opponent can easily move his hips and also can free the grip by kicking the legs.

2 Rodrigo will pass to his left so he swings his right leg back, putting his body weight on the left leg and pulls Shawn's pants down and to the right, driving the legs in the same direction as he takes a step forward with the right leg. Note that Rodrigo steps with the foot right next to Shawn's right hip, driving his right knee next to Shawn's right thigh. Once he plants the right foot with the knee touching the thigh, Rodrigo steps out with the left foot and pushes off it, leaning his body to the right.

3 Rodrigo returns to the center by stepping back with the left leg so the foot lines up with Shawn's right hip. He then steps back around with the right leg so his feet and body are positioned directly in front of Shawn's legs.

4 Rodrigo continues the drill by doing the same move to his right. He swings the left leg back, pushes Shawn's legs to the left and steps forward with his left leg, driving his knee onto Shawn's left thigh. Rodrigo then steps out with the right leg and leans his body to his left. To complete the pass Rodrigo would either drop his knees next to Shawn's left side with his chest pressing on top of Shawn's chest at a 90° angle or Rodrigo would put his knee on Shawn's stomach and go right to the knee on the stomach position.

Guard pass drill 2: Toreana with knee drop

One of the problems that can occur when using the toreana pass is that if the move is not executed quickly or if your opponent reacts quickly, he can take advantage of your pulling on his legs to drive them down to the mat and sit up. Once he sits up he can use his hands to move his hips and block your pass, or he can use them to pull your arm and do an arm-drag. This variation of the toreana deals with that problem by simply driving the legs to the side and sliding your knee between his legs so he can't continue rolling to the side and turn to all fours. This drill will help you master this important variation.

1 Rodrigo stands in front of Shawn while holding the gi pants, ready to use the toreana. Rodrigo steps out with his left leg as he pushes Shawn's legs to the right. Rodrigo lifts his right foot off the mat and quickly steps forward with it, dropping the right knee between Shawn's legs and knees with his left knee next to Shawn's left shoulder. Rodrigo places his left hand on Shawn's left shoulder to prevent him from rolling over to his left and turning to all fours to defend the pass.

1 Detail: Notice in this demonstration that Rodrigo's right hand pushes Shawn's left knee down and to the left while the left hand pushes the right shoulder down in the opposite direction. This not only prevents Shawn from turning to all fours but also freezes his hips, limiting any movement.

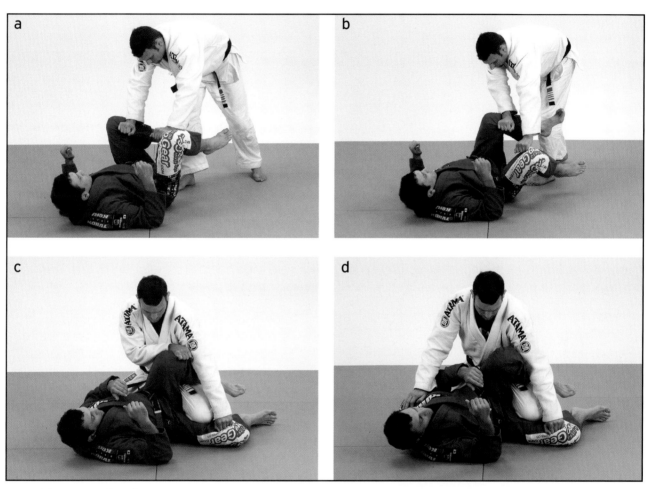

2 Rodrigo repeats the drill to the right side: he steps out with the right leg, pushes Shawn's legs to the left and drops his left knee between Shawn's legs. Rodrigo kneels down next to Shawn's left side and places his right hand on the left shoulder.

Guard pass drill 3: Toreana with knee drop, opponent rolls

A continuation of the previous drill is to actually allow the opponent to roll to his knees and then take his back. This situation may occur because you are slow to place your hand on his shoulder to stop him from rolling or because you actually want to allow him to roll to take the back. If you practice this drill you will be a master at taking people's backs. We pick up the drill from the moment Rodrigo drops his knee between Shawn's legs.

The best way to practice these three guard pass drills is to start with #85, then after you have done at least 10 repetitions go to drill #86, then drill #87 in sequence. These three drills build off each other and increase in difficulty.

1 Rodrigo pushes Shawn's legs to the left and drops his left knee between Shawn's legs. This time, however, he doesn't place his right hand on Shawn's left shoulder, either because he is late or because he wants him to roll so he can take his back. Shawn rolls to his right. Notice Rodrigo's right hand is planted on the mat wide to keep his torso up so he can move quickly.

2 As Shawn starts to roll to his right Rodrigo wraps his left arm around Shawn's chest to control the speed of the roll. With his left arm wrapped around Shawn's chest Rodrigo can slow him down by leaning his weight to his right (away from the direction of the roll) or by following Shawn's body as he rolls. If Rodrigo doesn't do either Shawn may simply roll too fast for Rodrigo to take the back and end up on all fours. As Rodrigo allows Shawn to roll, but at a slower pace, he slides his right foot along the mat right next to Shawn's right hip. As Shawn continues to turn, his hips come off the mat and Rodrigo can hook his right leg on Shawn's right leg for the first hook.

3 Having already hooked Shawn's right leg, Rodrigo loops the left leg around Shawn's back and hooks the heel in front of Shawn's left hip for the second hook. Notice that Rodrigo uses his right arm to help his body move – he pushes off it when he wants to throw his body over Shawn's and he bends the arm and leans to the right when he want to slow Shawn's rolling action. At the end of the move Rodrigo can simply release the right hand from the mat and slide it under Shawn's neck and grab the left collar, setting up a choke.

2 **Reverse angle of the motion:** Notice how Rodrigo pushes off his right arm to move his body as he slides his right knee along the ground aiming towards Shawn's right hip. As soon as Shawn's hips raise off the ground Rodrigo slides the knee and the leg under Shawn's leg.

Standing guard pass: Stacking

Rodrigo here demonstrates one of the most effective and traditional methods of guard passing in Gracie Jiu-Jitsu, the stacking method. In this case Rodrigo uses the standing stack but the same method can be used without standing up.

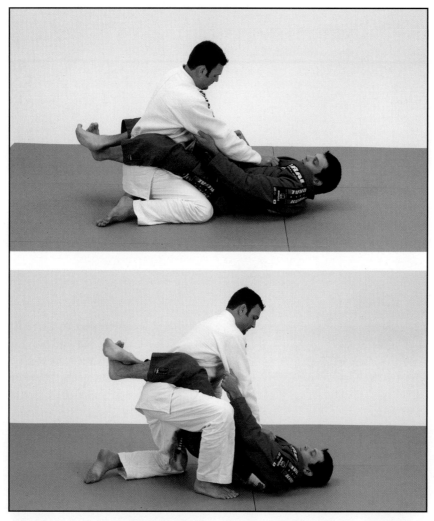

1 Rodrigo is in Shawn's closed guard with good posture. Rodrigo presses down on his left hand, further pinning Shawn's hips as he steps out with his right leg, planting the foot next to Shawn's left hip. Notice the position of Rodrigo's left leg: the knee is down with the leg opened straight back.

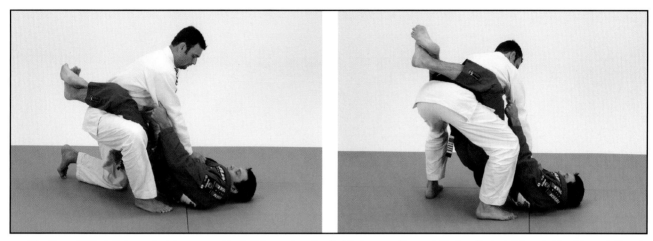

2 Pivoting off his left knee Rodrigo opens the left leg out and puts his toes on the mat. Notice that at this point Rodrigo's left and right legs are pointing in the same direction, diagonal to Shawn's hips. Rodrigo's weight is equally distributed between his legs and both his arms pin Shawn's hips and torso to the mat. Rodrigo is not leaning forward; his weight is centered through his torso and legs. Pushing off his feet, Rodrigo stands up. Notice that Rodrigo stood up without moving the left foot from where it was planted before; he simply pushed up and pivoted off the toes, aiming his left knee out. Again look at Rodrigo's weight distribution: not forward and not back but centered. His back is straight. Rodrigo arches back with his torso while pushing off his arm, forcing Shawn to open his legs and break the closed guard.

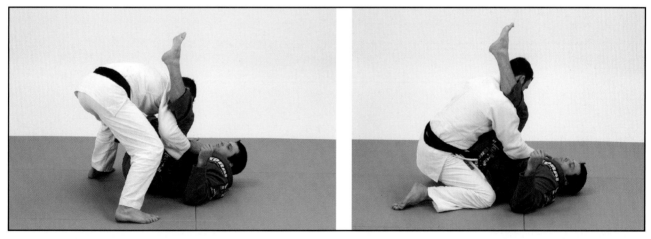

3 Having broken Shawn's legs open, Rodrigo drops his hips slightly and because he had his right foot forward, hooks his right arm under Shawn's left leg (should Rodrigo have stepped first with the left foot, he would have his left foot forward and then would have to use his left arm to underhook Shawn's right leg). At this point Rodrigo's left arm is bent with his forearm pressing against Shawn's right leg to prevent him from pulling it and attempt to triangle Rodrigo. Rodrigo drops his knees down to the mat with his hips next to Shawn's hips. Rodrigo reaches with his right hand and grabs Shawn's right collar and switches his left hand to grab the back of Shawn's pants.

4 Rodrigo pushes off his left leg while keeping his right knee on the mat and pulls up on his right arm as he drives his shoulders against Shawn's legs, stacking them over his head. Rodrigo then turns his shoulders to the left, pivoting around Shawn's left leg and driving his legs over to the side as Rodrigo kneels with both knees next to Shawn's body, having successfully passed the guard.

Incorrect:

Rodrigo grabs the collar with the thumb pointing down and the fingers on the outside, causing his elbow to be open. Shawn uses the left hand to push open Rodrigo's right arm and escapes the control, bringing the left leg down and the knee under the arm.

Reverse Angle Details:

(a) Notice Shawn's feet and hip position as he stands up. His hips are turned so he has balance in all directions.

(b) Rodrigo arches his hips back to break Shawn's lock.

(c & d) As Rodrigo circles his right arm around Shawn's left leg his left forearm presses against Shawn's right thigh to prevent him from pulling the arm forward to execute a triangle.

(e & f) Rodrigo opens Shawn's right lapel with his left hand and grabs it with his right, making sure to grab with the fingers in and the thumb pointing up to help keep his right elbow close and tight against Shawn's leg.

(g & h) Rodrigo uses his left hand to grab the back of Shawn's pants as he pushes off his left foot stacking Shawn's legs over his head. Rodrigo twists his shoulders right to left, clearing Shawn's legs, and drives his chest against them, pushing them aside.

a

a

b

c

d

e

f

g

h

Passing the guard

In this technique Rodrigo demonstrates an important concept when passing the guard. In this case he uses the knee through method to show the importance of keeping the opponent's back flat. Rodrigo may end up there as he is trying to pass the guard and gets caught in the half-guard or he may use it from the standing pass. In the latter case, Rodrigo needs to use his weight and head and shoulder position to keep Shawn's back flat on the ground. Here, we start from the half-guard.

Concept #1: Keep the opponent's back and hips flat on the mat: Knee through method

1 Rodrigo demonstrates the knee through pass keeping Shawn's back flat. Rodrigo gets caught in Shawn's half-guard with his right leg trapped between Shawn's legs. Rodrigo wraps his right arm under Shawn's left arm while making sure he puts his weight on his right shoulder and pressing it against Shawn's left shoulder to keep him flat on the mat. Rodrigo opens his left leg out and pushes off his foot to add pressure to his chest and shoulders as he uses his left hand to push Shawn's right knee down. Rodrigo slides his left leg between Shawn's legs until his knee clears the lock, leaving only his foot trapped by Shawn's legs.

2 Rodrigo moves his left hand from Shawn's knee to grab the right elbow. Rodrigo pulls up on Shawn's right elbow to add pressure to his pass and to keep Shawn's back flat on the mat. Rodrigo continues to drive his hips forward until his left foot escapes Shawn's legs. Rodrigo ends up passing Shawn's guard and is in side control with his hips facing forward. Notice that at all times Rodrigo uses his weight, his body position, and grips to keep Shawn flat on his back.

Concept # 2: Control the outside knee

Many times when passing the guard, the passer tries to control the inside knee in the belief that he will control the opponent's body. That is incorrect. When you control the inside knee only the opponent still has his hips free and can easily turn towards you.

Incorrect: Rodrigo is on Shawn's left side. Even when he is controlling Shawn's inside knee (in this case, his left knee), Shawn is still able to turn to his left to face Rodrigo, escape the hips and replace the guard.

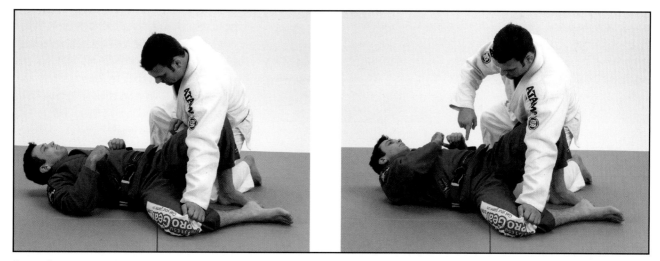

Correct: Rodrigo again is on Shawn's left but this time he grabs and pins Shawn's outside knee (here, the right knee) to the mat, freezing his hips and preventing Shawn from turning his body towards Rodrigo.

Butterfly guard pass 1: Arm-lock

Rodrigo here utilizes a guard pass to illustrate how pinning the opponent's outside knee to the mat forces him to face away from the side he will pass. If the opponent is able to turn in he can better defend and replace the guard.

1 Rodrigo is in Shawn's butterfly guard. He controls Shawn's right knee by pinning it to the mat with his left hand. His right hand is on Shawn's left knee. Rather than pass to his left, in which case Shawn could easily turn to that side and face Rodrigo, Rodrigo instead passes to the opposite side while pinning Shawn's right knee to the mat. This prevents Shawn from turning to his left side and facing Rodrigo as he passes. Rodrigo pushes Shawn's left knee to the left with his right hand and steps forward with his left leg, sliding his knee on top of Shawn's left leg.

2 Rodrigo continues sliding his left knee around Shawn's left leg until he has knee on the stomach. Since Shawn's pinned knee prevents him from turning his body to face Rodrigo, he uses his left arm to try to block Rodrigo from reaching side-control. While still pinning Shawn's right knee to the mat with his left hand, Rodrigo pulls Shawn's left arm up with his right arm deflecting the block. He hops forward with his right foot and further slides his left knee on Shawn's chest. At this point Rodrigo has a lot of his weight on his left hand and knee, making it easy for him to pivot around these two points.

a | b | c

3 Rodrigo quickly pivots his body on his left knee until he can step with his right leg over Shawn's head, placing the foot next to Shawn's right ear. At the same time Rodrigo releases his left hand grip from Shawn's right knee and wraps his arm around Shawn's left arm, setting up the arm-lock. Rodrigo drops his back to the mat and extends Shawn's arm. Rodrigo grabs the wrist with both hands and thrusts his hip up against the elbow joint for the arm-lock. Notice how Rodrigo closed his left knee in towards his right, taking away any space for Shawn to pull his arm out.

Butterfly guard pass 2: Hip turn

Utilizing the same concept of pinning one side and passing to the opposite side, Rodrigo this time uses a simple hip turn to clear Shawn's hooks from his butterfly guard and reach side control.

1 Rodrigo is in Shawn's butterfly guard. Shawn has his right knee on the ground. He wraps his left hand between Rodrigo's right arm and torso while using his left foot, hooked under Rodrigo's right thigh, to control and even perhaps lift and sweep him. This is a classic butterfly guard set-up. Rodrigo uses his left hand to pin Shawn's right knee to the mat to set up the pass to the opposite side.

2 Rodrigo grabs the back of Shawn's gi with his right hand and turns his hips in a counter-clockwise direction using his leg to deflect Shawn's left leg towards the left. Rodrigo drives his right knee under Shawn's left leg, further forcing Shawn towards his right knee and away from Rodrigo. At this point Rodrigo has effectively passed Shawn's guard.

3 Rodrigo continues to pin Shawn's right knee to the mat keeping him from turning towards his own left. Rodrigo presses his chest against Shawn's chest pining him to the mat and reaching side control. Rodrigo's right hand pushes Shawn's gi to the mat forcing him flat and his right shoulder presses against Shawn's left chin to keep him from being able to turn his head to the left as well making it virtually impossible for Shawn to turn into Rodrigo to escape the side control.

Butterfly guard pass 3: Jump over

In this case Rodrigo uses a different method of passing the butterfly guard. Here, he is able to push Shawn's back to the mat. This is a mistake on Shawn's part, because with his back on the ground his hooks have limited range of control as his legs cannot follow Rodrigo's hips throughout the full range of motion. Rodrigo takes advantage of that and jumps over Shawn's hook for the pass.

1 Shawn has Rodrigo in his butterfly guard with his left foot hooked on Rodrigo's right thigh. This time however Rodrigo is able to push Shawn's back flat on the mat. Rodrigo underhooks his right arm under Shawn's left arm places his head on the right side of Shawn's head and drives his right shoulder on Shawn's left shoulder. Rodrigo uses his left hand to pin Shawn's right knee to the mat preventing him from turning his body towards the left. At this point Rodrigo has most of his weight on his head and shoulders.

2 Rodrigo pushes off his feet and launches his legs up in the air, clearing Shawn's hook. Since Shawn cannot turn to his own left, at most he can extend his left leg straight up but that will not be sufficient to continue to use his left foot hook and prevent Rodrigo from jumping over it. Rodrigo keeps his legs straight up over his head.

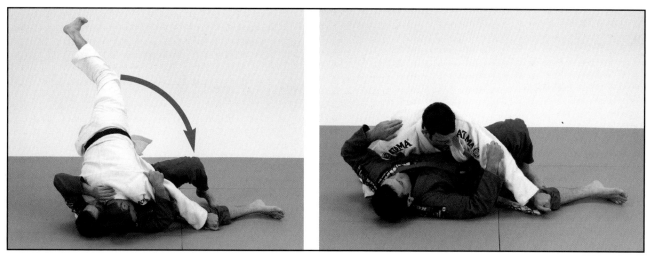

3 Rodrigo turns his body to his right. First his left foot lands next to Shawn's left side, then the right foot. He then brings his knees in next to Shawn's left side having passed the guard. Notice again that Rodrigo uses many of the guard passing concepts previously explained as he pins Shawn's back flat to the ground and doesn't release his right knee forcing his body not only to be flat but also keeping Shawn from turning into Rodrigo.

3 **Incorrect:** If Rodrigo doesn't pin Shawn's right leg away from the side he is passing, Shawn can easily replace the guard by sliding the left knee in front of Rodrigo's hips and looping the right leg over Rodrigo's head.

KNEE ON THE STOMACH

The knee on the stomach is a dynamic position from which you can launch many submission attacks. Because it is a dynamic position it is also a very unstable position – you need to rely on movement and weight adjustment to maintain control of your opponent.

In the knee on the stomach, you have one leg pressing down on top of your opponent's waist while the other is open wide to maintain both your balance and pressure on the opponent's body. Additionally, you will use your hands to grab the opponent's gi to help increase the pressure of your knee.

The knee on the stomach is a position that creates a great deal of discomfort for the opponent, undermining his resistance and forcing him at times to hastily attempt an escape, giving you opportunities for submission.

Do's:

- Keep your outside leg semi-flexed so you can easily adjust your foot position (figure A).
- Apply pressure by putting much of your body weight on the knee pressing on the stomach.
- Pull up on your hand grips to add even more pressure to the stomach.
- Be ready to move and adjust your position at all times in response to your opponent's reactions.

Don'ts:

- Don't put your outside knee on the ground; this will decrease much of the pressure on your opponent (figure B).
- Don't put the foot of the knee on the stomach on the ground. Again, this reduces the pressure and will slow you down.
- Don't lean too far forward or back.
- Don't keep your head so near your opponent that he can grab your collar and pull you down.

FIGURE A

FIGURE B

Achieving knee on the stomach

Properly reaching a position is as important as being able to attack
from that position. Rodrigo here gives a few tips on the proper way
to reach the knee on the stomach.

1 Rodrigo grabs Shawn's belt at the left side of his hip with
the right hand and places his right forearm across Shawn's
hips. Rodrigo pushes down on the right elbow so his forearm
presses down and pins Shawn's hips, allowing him to slide his
knee across the stomach. Notice Rodrigo points to the detail
of his right elbow pressing down. Normally Rodrigo's left arm
would be wrapped behind Shawn's head for control.

2 Pushing off his arms, Rodrigo springs up on his feet while
sliding the right knee right in front of his right forearm until
the knee reaches the outside of Shawn's hips. Rodrigo opens the
left leg out with the foot planted away from Shawn but not so
far that the leg can't remain flexed.

3 Rodrigo's left hand continues to grab
behind Shawn's neck while the right
one still grabs the belt. Notice that
Rodrigo pulls up on his hands while pressing down on his right knee to add pressure on Shawn's stomach.

3 **Alternative grip:** Rodrigo uses an
alternative grip here with his left hand
grabbing behind Shawn's head and the right
grabbing Shawn's gi pants at the right
knee. The advantage of this grip is that you
take away the opponent's ability to move
since he cannot use his right leg to push.
However, you are not in a good position to
attack. This is a good grip to assert your
control in a street fight and to undermine
your opponent's resolve in a match or to
score points in a Jiu-Jitsu match (when you
have to maintain the position for 3 seconds
before points are counted).

3 **Alternative grip:** With this grip,
Rodrigo uses his left hand to grab
Shawn's right sleeve at the elbow and the
right hand to grab inside the right collar.
This is a great position for an arm-lock or
a choke since the right is hand already in
position for the choke and the left hand is
pulling up on Shawn's right arm. This is a
little less stable than the other grips so
you have to be more aware of the opponent's escape attempts.

Knee on the stomach to arm-lock

One of the most common attacks from the knee on the stomach is the arm-lock to the far arm. As the opponent struggles to escape the discomfort of having the knee pressing on his stomach, he tries to use the hand on the far arm to push the knee away. This can leave a gap between his elbow and his body, thus exposing the arm for the submission.

1 Rodrigo has his right knee on Shawn's stomach and is applying pressure. Shawn uses his left hand to try to push the knee away and escape the position, but his elbow is out, creating a gap for Rodrigo to exploit.

a · b · c

2 Rodrigo inserts his right hand, palm facing up, into the gap between Shawn's elbow and torso, grabbing Shawn's left triceps. Rodrigo pulls up on Shawn's arm, pulling Shawn toward him. Pulling Shawn turns him onto his right side makes for a shorter distance that Rodrigo has to travel around Shawn's torso for the arm-lock. It also allows Rodrigo to control Shawn's arm and keep him from escaping. With his left hand Rodrigo pushes on the back of Shawn's left shoulder both to continue the turn and for extra control.

2 Detail: Notice how Rodrigo's right arm is bent with the elbow touching his own stomach for extra power in pulling Shawn's arm. Also notice how Rodrigo cradles Shawn's arm between his hand and the crease of his elbow so Shawn cannot pull his arm away.

3 Rodrigo extends his legs and steps around Shawn's head with his left leg. As his foot lands next to Shawn's back, Rodrigo grabs Shawn's left pant leg with his left hand to prevent Shawn from turning back towards his left and into Rodrigo, which would allow Shawn to pull his arm out. Notice that Rodrigo continues to pull up on Shawn's left arm at all times. Also notice how Rodrigo keeps his legs close together with the knees almost touching each other to trap the arm.

4 Rodrigo then sits down right next to Shawn's left shoulder. The combination of Rodrigo's left shin touching Shawn's left side of the torso and the right calf over the top of his head prevents Shawn from turning either in or out. Rodrigo leans back and extends Shawn's arm for the arm-lock. Notice that Rodrigo does not let go of his grip on Shawn's left leg even as he completes the arm-lock. This prevents Shawn from planting the leg on the ground to push and escape the submission.

Details:

Rodrigo shows that when Shawn has his back on the mat he has a longer distance to travel with his left leg to reach the opposite side.

As Shawn turns to his right Rodrigo points to the exact spot his left foot needs to land. He indicates the importance of having Shawn's body turned with the elbow almost at the highest point for a shorter distance that his left foot has to travel to reach that spot.

Rodrigo demonstrates the correct way to step over Shawn's body. By keeping his hips low and close to Shawn's arm and shoulder, he takes away any space for Shawn to pull his arm out of the grip.

Rodrigo demonstrates a common incorrect way to step over: with his legs extended, his hips are far from Shawn's shoulder, leaving a big gap Shawn can use to pull his arm out.

MOUNTED POSITION

Being mounted on your opponent is a great position to be in. From here only good things should happen as you have one of the best positions to inflict damage on your opponent. In a street fight you are in prime position to deliver strikes like punches and elbows to his face. In a Jiu-Jitsu match you have a variety of chokes & arm-locks available to submit your opponent. The mount however can be a very difficult position for one to maintain as your opponent has the power of his legs and hips to move you off him. If you act in haste you may well give him the chance to escape by sliding under your legs (elbow escape) or even worse reversing you with an upa (technique #12), ending up on the bottom inside your opponent's guard.

The most important thing you should do once you achieve the mount is to maintain it at all costs. Position your hips as far from your opponent's hips as possible to diminish the power of his bridging. Open your arms to stop any attempt to roll you over, even if you have to give up an attack! Most of the time it is better to let go of a choke and maintain the position rather than risk being reversed.

Choking stances to maintain base in the mount:
High stance (figure 1): Rodrigo places his right hand inside Shawn's collar while using the left arm with the hand planted out and above Shawn's shoulder and his weight shifted to the left to maintain his base. The high stance is the best option for the double attack, when you go for the choke and transition to the arm-lock if the opponent defends. Low stance (figure 2): Alternatively if Rodrigo wants to stay low for a more stable base, he lowers his torso while opening the left elbow out so his forearm is above Shawn's right shoulder and shifts his weight to the left side. The low stance opens up different attack possibilities, like the ezequiel choke.

However, you cannot just maintain the mount forever without creating dangerous situations for your opponent. If he is to remain calm and not feel threatened at all times he can and will concentrate all of his efforts to escape the position. By introducing the threat of a submission you will create the danger and a distraction, forcing him to divide his attention between defending the attack and escaping the position – opening up many opportunities for a submission attempt to work or to switch to another attack.

FIGURE 1

FIGURE 2

Mounted position drill 1: Roll and take the back

A great drill for the mounted position and for taking the back is shown here. In this drill Rodrigo not only exercises maintaining the mount as the opponent rolls over, a common occurrence when you mount a novice or someone without ground fighting skills on the street, but he also practices taking the back with hooks as the opponent rolls. Taking the back with hooks can occur from the mount as demonstrated here or from side control or passing the guard as the opponent rolls away to avoid the position.

1 Rodrigo starts the drill mounted on Shawn with his hands planted on the ground slightly wider apart than his shoulders.

2 As Shawn rolls to his left, Rodrigo simply follows him in the same direction by moving his hands to the right while opening the knees around Shawn just enough to be able to follow him without giving space for him to escape. It is important for Rodrigo not to clamp his knees on Shawn's body, otherwise he will roll over and lose the mount as Shawn rolls over. Shawn ends up flat on his stomach.

3 Continuing with the drill, as Shawn continues in his attempt to escape he pushes off his elbows and legs and tries to go to his knees. Rodrigo leans forward, placing more of his weight on his hands, and slides his feet in front of Shawn's hips for the hooks. Once he has the hooks in place Rodrigo wraps his arms around Shawn's chest just under his armpits and extends his body, driving his hips towards the mat forcing Shawn flat on the mat again.

Reverse View:

Notice Rodrigo's footwork as Shawn reverses and rolls back to his right. Rodrigo moves his hands to the right. To follow and maintain his position Rodrigo has to open the left leg out (the one farthest from the direction of the roll) placing the knee on the ground and lifting the foot. He then shifts his weight to his toes and lifts the left knee. As Shawn continues his roll to the right Rodrigo drops the left knee back to the mat and loops the foot over Shawn's right leg, ending up on the mount. It is *extremely important* to master this footwork, otherwise Shawn would have been able to trap Rodrigo's left leg and place him in the half-guard.

Mounted position drill 2: Transition to the side-mount

The positions in Gracie Jiu-Jitsu are not static positions. In fact, the strength of Gracie Jiu-Jitsu is in the transitions, in the ability of the fighter to adjust and mold his body to deflect the opponent's power and to use his weight distribution and body pressure to control his opponent. The mount is perhaps the least stable position in all of Jiu-Jitsu, therefore it is very important to be able to adjust to the ever-changing environment that your opponent presents if you are going to be successful at the mount. In this drill Rodrigo demonstrates the transition from the mount to the side-mount. The side-mount is a very good position to launch attacks such as the armlock and the double attack. This is another alternative to use when the opponent starts to roll to one side to escape the mount. Maintaining the position is key to being able to successfully attack from any position, and the mount is no different. Once you are good at maintaining the mount your opponent, in his struggle to escape, will yield openings for you to exploit.

1 Rodrigo begins the drill mounted on Shawn with the hands planted on the ground slightly wider apart than his shoulders.

2 Shawn starts to roll to his left, so Rodrigo leans forward, putting more of his weight on his hands and allowing his lower body to move more freely. Rodrigo starts shifting his left knee forward towards Shawn's head. At the same time Rodrigo raises his right knee off the mat until his foot is planted and the knee is perpendicular to the ground. Rodrigo uses his left arm to help move his torso towards Shawn's head while his right arm wraps around Shawn's right arm, setting up a possible arm-lock.

3 Shawn returns to the starting position with his back on the ground and this time turns to his right. Rodrigo repeats the move to reach the side-mount. The key to this move is the weight shift and the hip rotation to the same side so that the knee moves all the way to the partner's head.

Mounted position: Choke

The basic collar is the staple attack from the mounted position. If your opponent doesn't pay proper respect and dedicate enough effort to defend it you will simply finish the fight with the submission. Also, whenever the opponent attempts an elbow escape, one of the most common escapes used, he opens himself for the choke. So look for opportunities to use the choke and master it, and you will have an even stronger mounted position.

1 Rodrigo is mounted on Shawn with his right hand gripping Shawn's right collar.

2 Rodrigo twists his shoulders to the right and uses the left hand to grab Shawn's gi at the left shoulder.

3 Since he used his *right* hand to grab the collar first, the right forearm ends up under the left so Rodrigo drops his head to the *right*, drops his hips down pressing against Shawn's hips and pulls his elbows up tightening Shawn's collar around the neck for the choke. So remember the "right-right" key: If your *right* hand grips the collar first, your head goes to the *right*.

Mounted position: Elbow escape counter: Choke

Whenever you are mounted on your opponent and have one hand in the collar and he starts to use the elbow escape, it is your key to immediately counter it with a choke.

1 Rodrigo is mounted on Shawn with his right hand gripping Shawn's right collar.

2 Shawn begins to use the elbow escape to try to escape from the mount. Since Rodrigo has his right hand in the collar Shawn cannot turn to his right, or he will choke himself against Rodrigo's right forearm, so the only option for the elbow escape is to the left. Shawn turns his body left, and inserts his left elbow between his ribs and Rodrigo's right leg. Shawn extends the left leg as he continues to turn to the left in his escape attempt.

3 Rodrigo immediately twists his shoulders to the right while using his left hand to grab Shawn's gi on the left shoulder as close to the neck as possible. He drops his head to his right and applies the choke as he expands his chest and pulls his elbows up, tightening Shawn's collar around his neck.

4 Alternatively, when Shawn starts the elbow escape Rodrigo can switch his body position by sliding his hips to Shawn's right side. Raising the right leg so his foot locks onto Shawn's left hip and sliding the left knee up towards Shawn's head sets up the double attack.

Mounted Position: Double attack choke: Arm-lock

Early in your Jiu-Jitsu career single direct attacks are the only thing you can muster, but as you progress in the sport and fight against more advanced opponents you will realize that you need to combine attacks in order to be effective. The double attack choke - arm-lock from the mount is one of the most basic yet most effective of these combinations.

1 Rodrigo is mounted on Shawn. He sets up the double attack by first going for the choke. Rodrigo grabs Shawn's right collar with his right hand.

2 Rodrigo plants his left hand out past Shawn's head for balance. Shawn uses his left hand to grab and pull open Rodrigo's right wrist to release the pressure on his neck from Rodrigo's right forearm. Rodrigo quickly attacks with the choke; he twists his shoulders to the right and grabs Shawn's gi at the left shoulder to complete the choke grip.

3 Shawn counters by sliding his left forearm just inside Rodrigo's left forearm to block the choke. Rodrigo then slides his left knee up towards Shawn's head as he moves his hips to the left. Notice that at this point Rodrigo's hips are trapping Shawn's right arm.

4 Rodrigo uses his left hand to pull up on Shawn's left arm creating the space for his right leg to tuck under the arm while he starts to lean to the right and away from Shawn's head with his body. Rodrigo then switches and uses the left hand to grab on Shawn's gi at the left shoulder and wraps Shawn's right arm with his own right arm making sure he doesn't alert Shawn to the attack by pulling up on the arm. Rodrigo leans further to the right and back to allow his left leg to circle around and over Shawn's head. As soon as his left foot touches the mat Rodrigo starts to fall back as he extends his body and thrusts his hips up against Shawn's right elbow hyperextending the joint for the arm-lock. Here again the "right-right" key applies: your *right* hand grips the collar first so you will attack his *right* arm.

Escaping the mount: Opponent holds one or both wrists

Hopefully you will never find yourself on the bottom with the opponent mounted on you, but in the dynamics of a street fight or in a Jiu-Jitsu match situations like that occur. A common occurrence in a street fight when the opponent is mounted on you is for him to hold both your wrists down, pinning them against the ground. In Jiu-Jitsu matches that is not so common, although it still may occur, since pinning one or both wrists is a set up for the Americana attack. Rodrigo here demonstrates how to escape the position with a slight variation of the upa escape (technique #20).

1 Shawn is mounted on Rodrigo pinning both of Rodrigo's wrists against the mat.

2 Rodrigo loops his left foot over Shawn's right foot and plants it on the ground, trapping Shawn's right leg, and bridges by thrusting his hips up. Notice how far forward Shawn's shoulders moved because of Rodrigo's bridging. Now Shawn's weight is transferred to his hands.

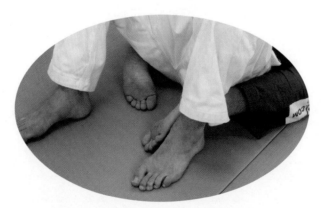

2 **Detail:** Notice Rodrigo's foot placement: he keeps his left foot right next to Shawn's right foot, not allowing any space for the foot to slip out of the trap.

3 At the height of the bridge Rodrigo turns his torso to his left, shifting more of Shawn's weight on his right hand and less on the left one. This allows Rodrigo to reach over with his own right hand and grab Shawn's right wrist with it. At this point Rodrigo has trapped Shawn's right side (the right foot blocked by Rodrigo's left foot and the right arm blocked by Rodrigo's right hand) taking away any option for Shawn to reach out and brace himself to prevent Rodrigo from rolling him over to Shawn's right. Rodrigo ends up in Shawn's guard having escaped the mount.

Front view:

Notice Rodrigo's mechanics to free his right arm: As he bridges right he transfers more of Shawn's weight over to the right hand making Shawn's left side lighter. Notice that instead of trying to push Shawn's left arm away with his right arm, which would require more strength, Rodrigo lifts his right elbow up, pivoting off his right wrist and driving his right arm up and around his head to the left until he can reach Shawn's right wrist with his own right hand.

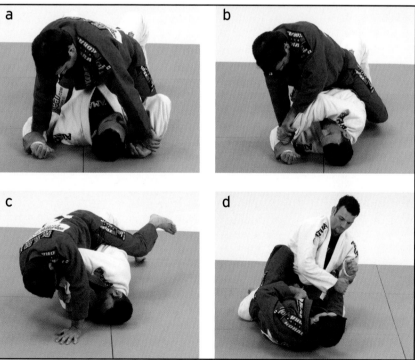

ESCAPING THE BACK

Being able to maintain your wits and escape even the worst situation is invaluable in life, especially in a street fight. In Gracie Jiu-Jitsu there is no worse situation than having your opponent on your back with hooks on ready to choke you. At this point calmness, clear thinking, and confidence in your ability to defend yourself and ultimately escape the position willl allow you to succeed in your quest to escape the back and regain equal or better than equal position in relation to your opponent.

When faced with this situation your first concern is always to survive the attack and protect your neck and only then try to escape the back control. Do not rush to escape and allow your opponent an opening to choke you. Take your time: defend, then escape!

Escaping the back 1: Opponent is blocked early

One of the worst positions one can be in in a fight is having someone on your back. Without being able to see the opponent's hands the defender has to rely on maintaining his calm and using perfect technique to survive and escape the position. Rodrigo here shows the exact way to properly use your weight, body position and mechanics to escape this most difficult position. With proper repetition and understanding of the mechanics of the escape you will

develop tremendous confidence in your ability to escape and be able to calmly react to the situation if it ever occurs. To fully master this technique Rodrigo recommends that you use this technique as a drill by starting with your opponent on your back wanting to submit you while your objective is to escape. Once you escape or if you are submitted you repeat the drill. In this first case Rodrigo is able to block the opponent's hand before he grabs the collar.

Defending the neck:
Notice that Rodrigo's first intention when trying to escape is to avoid being choked, so his total attention is directed to blocking the choke. Only when he has the opponent's hands in control and feels safe from a possible choke does he begin his move to escape the position.

1 Shawn is on Rodrigo's back with hooks on. Rodrigo crosses his arms in front of his chest with the hands open and palms facing out ready to capture any attacking hands. Since Rodrigo's hands are guarding his neck, any time Shawn slides his arm around the neck it will first be intercepted by Rodrigo's palm. Shawn's right hand approaches Rodrigo's neck and hits the left palm. Rodrigo grabs Shawn's right wrist and pushes it open, allowing him to slip his right arm under, knowing full well that Shawn will attack the neck with the other hand.

2 Rodrigo blocks the path to his neck and collar with his open right palm facing out and intercepts Shawn's left hand. Rodrigo grabs Shawn's left wrist and wraps his left arm over Shawn's left arm, trapping it. Rodrigo at this point can initiate his escape.

Escaping the back:

1 With Shawn's left arm trapped and unable to attack with a choke, Rodrigo knows that is the best side on which to initiate his escape. The first thing Rodrigo does is to get into proper position by moving his head to the left side of Shawn's head. Otherwise Shawn can block his escape simply by having his head on the left side of Rodrigo's, putting his head in position to block Rodrigo head. Rodrigo then shifts his weight to his left side by pushing off his right foot and leaning his body to the left.

2 Rodrigo's objective is to get his back flat on the ground with his weight on top of Shawn's left leg to prevent Shawn from pushing back and re-centering Rodrigo's body and regain back control. Notice that Rodrigo pushes off his right foot to press his back and head to the ground. It is a very common mistake when attempting to escape the back to curl up your body and legs. This is *wrong* as it makes you very light. All your weight is concentrated on your hips, allowing the opponent to easily drive your body back to the center. By pushing off the right foot, Rodrigo drives his head and back to the mat while his hips weigh down on Shawn's left thigh, making it virtually impossible for Shawn to push him back to center.

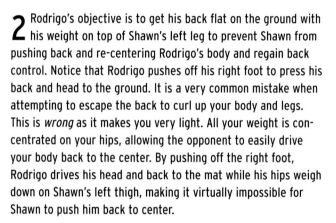

3 Rodrigo continues with his weight on his hips, back and head as he pushes off his feet, driving his body up towards Shawn's head. At this point, having lost the back control, Shawn may try to mount by looping the right leg over Rodrigo and turning his body over the top. Rodrigo uses his left hand to block Shawn's right leg from coming over. He uses the hip escape (see technique #1) to escape Shawn's mount attempt as he plants the left foot on the mat and pushes off it, escaping his hips to the left.

4 As Shawn struggles to come on top of Rodrigo, Rodrigo braces his right forearm in front of Shawn's hips to stop his progress. Rodrigo escapes his hips further out to the left, curls the right leg to slide the right knee up between Shawn's legs until the knee comes on the outside of Shawn's left hip.

5 Rodrigo continues to push off his feet and move away from Shawn with his hips escaping to the right until he can get his legs around Shawn's body and regain the closed guard.

Escaping the back incorrect:

Rodrigo begins to escape correctly but as he has his back on the ground he makes the common mistake of curling his body, putting his weight on his hips. Shawn can easily slide his left hand under Rodrigo's back and use his legs and arms to bring Rodrigo back to center and regain back control.

Escaping the back 2: Opponent grabs the collar

In this second escape from the back, Rodrigo is late blocking Shawn's hand from grabbing the collar. With one hand on the collar and the other under Rodrigo's armpit Shawn has the makings of a good choke. Rodrigo needs to have a clear understanding of what he needs to do and the calmness that only comes with knowledge and experience to escape such a dire situation. Again, Rodrigo rec-

ommends that you use this technique as a drill by having your opponent start on your back with the hand on the collar trying to submit you. If you escape or if he submits you, start over. It is important to have been in this situation repeatedly so you have the calm and clear vision of the escape otherwise you will become exasperated, panic and be submitted.

1 Shawn is on Rodrigo's back with his right arm around Rodrigo's neck and the hand grabbing Rodrigo's left collar. Shawn's left arm is under Rodrigo's left arm ready to complete the choking motion by either reaching behind Rodrigo's neck or grabbing the opposite collar. Quick recognition of the escape route will save precious milliseconds and be the difference between escaping or being submitted. Rodrigo needs to immediately recognize which is the proper side to escape. Should he choose the wrong side he will add to the choke pressure. Shawn's right hand is in the collar and points the way to the escape.

1a Shawn's right arm is around Rodrigo's neck. The right (choking) hand would grab the collar for the choke. The right hand indicates the direction of the escape.

1b Shawn's left arm is around Rodrigo's neck. The left (choking) hand points the direction of the escape.

2 With clear understanding of his direction of escape Rodrigo can proceed. He grabs Shawn's right arm with both hands, the right one at the triceps and the left one at the forearm pulling it down to relieve any pressure around his neck and to force his own body to the left. At the same time Rodrigo starts to lean back.

3 Rodrigo leans further back with his torso as he switches his head to the left side of Shawn's head to prevent Shawn from using the head to block Rodrigo's escape. Notice how Rodrigo presses his head against Shawn's left shoulder taking away any space Shawn could use to swing his head back around Rodrigo's head.

4 Pushing off his feet Rodrigo drives his shoulders and head towards the left until he has them on the mat. Once his head and shoulders touch the mat, Rodrigo starts sliding his hips to the left, making sure he keeps his weight on his back and on his hips. Should Rodrigo tense up and curl his body forward his weight would transfer to his hips, making it easy for Shawn to push him back to center and regain back control.

5 Now that Rodrigo has his full body on the mat, Shawn attempts to mount with his right leg. Rodrigo releases his hands from Shawn's right arm, instead using them to block Shawn's right leg to prevent the mount. From there Rodrigo would continue with the same motion as in the previous technique.

Escaping the back 3: Push and bridge

In the third escape, the opponent is quicker than you and he not only grabs the collar but in anticipation of your escape tips your body to the opposite side. In this case Shawn attacks Rodrigo's neck with his left hand so Rodrigo's escape would be to the right. This time however he is late in his reaction and Shawn drives him to the left, making it very difficult to use the previous escape. Note that the previous escape may still work but Rodrigo will have to swing his body all the way to the right to succeed and Shawn will try to

stop Rodrigo from doing that. In that case this escape from the back is the best option. Remember these three escapes are shown in order of anticipation. In the first one Rodrigo is able to block Shawn's hand from reaching his collar so he traps the arm and escapes. In the second case Shawn's hand reaches the collar so Rodrigo escapes in the direction the hand points to him. In the third, he is so late that Shawn has turned him to the opposite side of the normal escape so his only option is the push and bridge.

1 Shawn is on Rodrigo's back and his left arm wraps around Rodrigo's neck with the hand grabbing the collar. For illustration only Shawn's left hand points toward the normal direction for Rodrigo to escape.

2 Knowing Rodrigo's escape direction, Shawn is quicker in his reaction. He tips Rodrigo's body to the left while using his head on the right side of Rodrigo's head to block him from moving his body to the right for the normal escape. Shawn's reaction forces Rodrigo to use the push and bridge. Note that Shawn's left hand grabs Rodrigo's right collar while his right hand is under Rodrigo's right arm and grabs the left collar to pull down for the choke. With his right hand Rodrigo grabs Shawn's left sleeve at the forearm while his left hand grabs the back of Shawn's left sleeve just under the elbow.

3 Rodrigo pulls Shawn's left arm down with his right hand to release the choke slightly and create a little space between the arm and his neck. With his left hand Rodrigo braces under Shawn's left elbow. In one motion Rodrigo pushes off his feet to bridge his hips up and pull his body down and away while using his arms to push Shawn's left arm up, slipping his head from the left arm noose. Rodrigo pushes off his feet, pressing his back to the ground and dropping the weight of his hips on top of Shawn's left leg while driving the back of his head to the mat to prevent Shawn from wrapping his arm back around again.

4 Having escaped the choke, Rodrigo turns his body towards Shawn's and escapes his hips to the left to either replace the guard or try to gain top position, depending on Shawn's balance and reaction to the escape.

CONCLUSION

To become a Black Belt it is not necessary to have a massive arsenal of weapons but rather have solid tools you have mastered. At the highest levels, Gracie Jiu-Jitsu is not about who knows the most positions and techniques but rather who makes the best and quickest decisions and executes the technique with the proper mechanics.

Always keep an open mind and your path to the Black Belt will be interesting, challenging, fun and rewarding. Enjoy your training!